BABY-LED SLEEPING

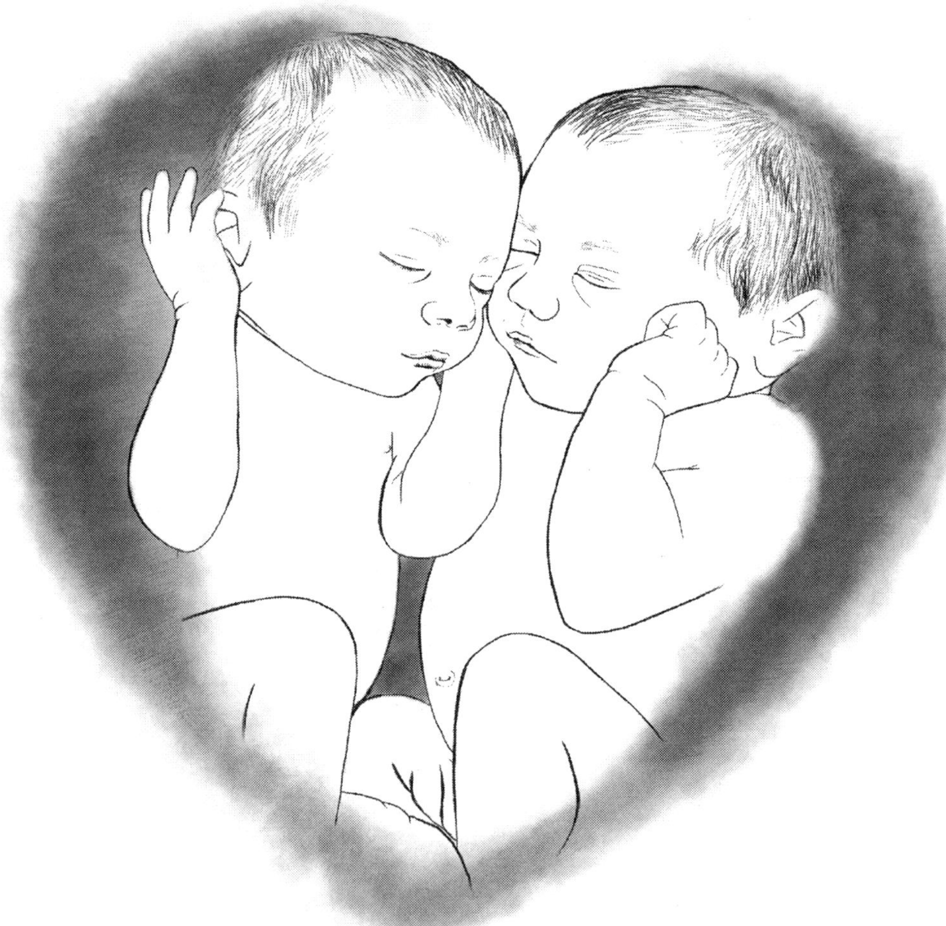

BABY-LED SLEEPING

How to Get Your Baby Sleeping.
The Gentle Way

HAZEL HAYWARD
Illustrated by Stephanie MacSorley

TINY TOES
PUBLISHING

First published by Tiny Toes Publishing in 2021

10 9 8 7 6 5 4 3 2 1

ISBN: 978-1-7399106-0-0

www.twinningituk.com

Illustrated by Stephanie MacSorley

Disclaimer
The information in this book has been provided as general guidance to the specific topics addressed, but it is not intended as a replacement or to be relied on for medical, healthcare or other professional advice. To the best of the author's knowledge the information given is correct and up-to-date at the time of publication. The author and publishers do not accept any responsibility for the use, or misuse, of content from this book.

I dedicate this book to my mum. For being there for me whenever I needed her, no matter what hour. Some of my earliest childhood memories from when I was four or five are of me calling out to her in the night and her being right there for me. I cannot remember now why I needed her, but I remember her being there and calming me and making everything OK. I wish she was still here to see my children grow up and I hope she would be proud of the values she has instilled in me.

I would like to thank my husband Jim for being so supportive when I spent every waking moment hidden away writing this book to help others, and also for the times he has got up in the night over the past couple of years to help with night feeds or just to give them a cuddle to get them back to sleep. We really do make a great team!

My sweet babies Maisie and Frankie who bring me so much joy every day and really are the greatest gift.

A really special thanks to the many families that have chosen me to support them when it comes to their baby's sleep issues. I learn so much from you as I hope you do from me. I hope this book helps many more families in the future to understand what their baby's needs are when it comes to sleep.

ABOUT THE AUTHOR

As a maternity nurse, sleep consultant and doula, I have always had a passion for the wellbeing of babies and their parents.

I am a certified sleep consultant who has helped many families directly, as well as a huge number indirectly via my social media channels.

I am a gentle sleep consultant, which means I take a very holistic approach when tackling sleep issues. I called this book "Baby-led Sleeping" not because I think your baby should be the ruler of the house when it comes to sleep, but because I find that learning to understand your baby's sleep needs and letting them lead you when it comes to their sleep needs is the most effective way of creating harmony for everyone.

Sleep has such an impact on our experience of being a parent. Babies manage fairly well on broken sleep but adults do not. So many people will tell you to nap when they nap, but by the time you have done the washing, tidied up your house a little, prepared meals and often cared for other children, before you know it there is rarely time to have a nap!

The early weeks, months (and years) can be exhausting, but when you learn how to handle your baby's sleep needs based on their behaviour and simple signs, it makes situations much easier to handle. Baby-led sleeping also means that you go at their pace, ensuring that their sleep needs are met.

As you learn about your baby's sleep needs, you will find a natural rhythm, which is predictable and allows for a more settled day for you, meaning more time to enjoy them.

I NEED YOU MUMMY

I need you mummy, I'm feeling cold
Please come to me and give me a hold

I need you mummy, my teeth really hurt
I'd rather be sleeping but feel so alert

I need you mummy, I'm feeling hungry
There's a growling noise coming from my tummy

I need you mummy, I'm not feeling sleepy
Please don't think I'm being needy

I need you mummy, I want your touch
Please come to me, I need you so much

I need you mummy, I heard a noise
And it definitely wasn't one of my toys

I need you mummy, I'm feeling sick
Please come mummy, please be quick

I need you mummy, I've woken up scared
Please stay with me mummy and stroke my hair

I need you mummy, just because
I'm only little and need your love

I'm coming my baby, I'm always near
No matter what hour it is, I am always here

HAZEL HAYWARD

CONTENTS

NO ONE KNOWS YOUR BABY AS WELL AS YOU

"They will sleep better if you stop holding them so much."
"They will sleep better if you give them a bottle."
"They will sleep better if you let them try and self settle."
"They will sleep better if you put them to bed at 7pm."
"They will sleep better if you leave them to cry."

Everyone loves to offer advice to the parents of a new baby. Some of it will be helpful, but you often need to take it with a pinch of salt. The truth is, when it comes to sleep, your situation is so individual, it is highly unlikely to be the same as a friend's, your mother's, or even that stranger in the supermarket.

All babies are different, and there is no one-size-fits-all when it comes to sleep. What works for one person won't necessarily work for another. Babies are not robots. We cannot programme them: there is no secret code. There are so many things that can influence the way a baby sleeps.

Don't ever let advice-givers make you feel inadequate. Nobody knows your situation or your baby better than you. Not me, not your friends, not your mother – and certainly not that stranger in the supermarket. You are the expert when it comes to your baby.

Of course, some advice can be useful – and the safety advice in the next section is crucial. However, where general tips can sometimes be worth a try, don't feel deflated if something that worked for your friend doesn't work for you. Their baby isn't YOUR baby, and believe me when I tell you that no two children are the same. I have worked with hundreds of parents of identical twins, and they can be polar opposites when it comes to sleep, even though they share the same DNA.

The key is to find the rhythm of your baby and work on the areas that you know you can influence (which you will find out from reading this book). Learn to understand areas you cannot change. Sleep will come in time, and if you work with your baby closely, you will find your way together.

In the blink of an eye they grow up and won't need you anymore during the night.

When I used to be up in the small hours feeling completely exhausted with my babies, to help get myself through, I would say to myself, "Is this the last time?"

"Is this the last time I will rock them to sleep?"

"Is this the last time they will let me sing to them?"

"Is this the last time they will let me feed them to sleep?"

There will always be a last time and you won't know when it is.

And as crazy as it sounds right now, when you are feeling sleep deprived, you may miss those magical moments when it is just you and them.

Chapter 1

SLEEP SAFETY

SAFE SLEEP

Before we talk about how to improve sleep, it is really important to go through safe sleep guidelines. These will ensure you provide the safest sleep environment and habits for your baby and help protect your baby against SIDS and anything else that could put them in danger.

SAME ROOM

Ideally, your baby should sleep in the same room as you for at least the first six months, and preferably twelve. Of course there may be a reason why this isn't possible, but do bear in mind that the safest place for them to sleep is close to their parent(s) in those first months. Please also bear in mind that they should be on a separate surface designed for infants. Bed-sharing significantly increases the risk of SIDS.[1,3]

SIDS

Before your anxiety moves into overdrive, remember that sudden infant death syndrome, often referred to as cot death, is **very rare**, though it worries so many new parents, fearful of the spectre of a sudden, unexplained death of an apparently healthy baby. In 2018, it very sadly affected 230 babies in the UK[2]. The risk of SIDS happening to your baby is **very low**, but it is nonetheless important to know how to put your baby down to sleep in a safe manner.

The cause of SIDS is unknown, but it may be due to a number of factors. It generally happens within the first six months of a baby's life and most often occurs with babies who have a low birth weight or were premature. The risk of SIDS can be significantly reduced by practising safe sleep guidelines. (Further research links about SIDS can be found at the rear of the book.)

"ALWAYS PUT YOUR BABY DOWN TO SLEEP ON THEIR BACK"

BABY ON BACK

Always put your baby down to sleep on their back, the safest way for a baby to sleep. Research has shown that since the guidance of sleeping a baby on their back came into place in 1992 and the launch of the Back to Sleep campaign in 1994 by NICHD (National Institute of Child Health & Development), SIDS cases have reduced by more than 80%.

Putting a baby down to sleep on their side or tummy is not safe. Do not take this risk. They sleep deeper on their tummies, which is thought to be one of the main contributing factors to incidences of SIDS. If a baby has an underlying condition or has issues caused by rebreathing expelled carbon dioxide, it is thought they may be in too deep a sleep to wake themselves up. Back sleeping is the safest way to protect your baby from SIDS.

I often come across people who say "but I slept on my tummy as a baby and I was fine" or "I laid my baby on their front and everything was OK". This may well have been the case, but there have been a few very sad cases where this has not been the outcome. And if you take one thing from this book, let it be this message.

Since the back to sleep campaign, positional plagiocephaly has become more common due to increased back sleeping. This condition is where the baby's head becomes flatter on one side or the back of the head due to the baby's preferred head position. To avoid this condition, consider alternating the baby's position in the cot from one end to the other (maintaining feet to foot – see diagram on next page), as it may be that they are turning their head in a certain direction to look at something in the room. Alternatively, if you know what it is that they are focusing on a lot, move the cot's position or whatever it is that has their attention.

Tummy time during the day when they are awake can be helpful so that the baby isn't constantly lying on their back. A baby's skull is very malleable. During the first one to two years they have two fontanelles – soft spots on the baby's head (one at the front, one at the back) that allow for growth. In the first couple of years the brain dramatically increases in size, after which the skull fuses, becoming less malleable. A lot of parents worry when their baby's head shape becomes flattened due to sleep positioning – and it can be quite pronounced in the first 12 months – but rest assured, once your baby becomes more upright during the day and they gain head control, the shape of their head should begin to become more symmetrical. If you are concerned this is not correcting itself, do speak with a healthcare professional.

Never use any type of wedge in a baby's cot to try and influence the way they position their heads.

FEET TO FOOT

Place your baby on their back in the cot with their feet at the foot. This is so that if they have a blanket over them, they cannot shuffle underneath it.

OPTIMUM TEMPERATURE

Try and keep the room between 16C and 20C. Dress your baby accordingly, so if it is cold in the room consider adding more layers of clothing.

EMPTY COT

Soft toys, loose blankets, comforters (soft blanket or scarf), or anything else that could pose a potential risk to your baby, should not be in the cot with them. The safest cot is an empty cot.

Dummies (pacifiers) are OK, but dummy clips must not be attached to dummies and left with a sleeping baby.

"BABIES QUICKLY LEARN THE LIMITS OF THEIR COT"

COT BUMPERS

Cot bumpers (even mesh varieties) are not advised, as babies can become caught up in them. Babies quickly learn the limits of their cot, and the consequence of getting caught up in a cot bumper is far greater than that of getting a limb caught in the bars. Babies usually move their limbs out of cot bars and very rarely injure themselves by getting an arm or leg stuck.[4] Manufacturers will have ensured the cot meets legal safety requirements so that the bars or panels are spaced between 50mm and 95mm apart – bigger gaps can trap a baby's head, arms or legs. And you can always check before purchasing.

NESTS/COCOONS

Use of sleep nests or cocoons, which are essentially mattresses with padded sides, are not recommended for any unattended sleep (no adult present in the room or present, but asleep). They can cause a baby to overheat or suffocate, due to their being on a soft surface rather than the recommended firm mattress. Soft mattresses, including those made of memory foam, could create an indentation and increase the chance of rebreathing (carbon dioxide expelled when a baby exhales is breathed back in again causing a reduction in oxygen in the blood). This can be very dangerous. Most babies' brains will trigger them to wake up and cry out if this happens, but some research suggests that babies who died from SIDS may have had a problem with the part of the brain that helps control breathing and did not wake when oxygen levels dropped due to rebreathing on a soft surface.[5]

From my experience, babies can also become very reliant on cocoons and nests, and it can be quite a task to take this away once they outgrow them. My advice would be to not start using them at all.

FIRM MATTRESS

Invest in a firm mattress with a waterproof cover that can be wiped down easily. A firm mattress helps with temperature control. Ensure that the mattress fits the sleep space properly so that there is no risk of the baby slipping down into a gap if the mattress is too small.

BLANKETS

Blankets, if used, should be tucked in firmly so they do not become loose. A cellular blanket is preferable, as it has tiny holes in it which allows for better air flow should a baby get it over their head. Ensure that any blanket that you use is not covering your baby past their shoulders. Ideally it should be under the level of their armpits so their arms are free. I would advise a baby sleep bag which is the correct size for the baby instead of using a blanket as there is less risk of it becoming loose within the cot like a blanket may.

PILLOWS & DUVETS

Pillows and duvets are unnecessary for babies and small children. They pose a suffocation risk. Avoid using them until your baby is at least two years old.[6]

SMOKING/E-CIGARETTES

Do not smoke around the baby and ensure that anyone who has been smoking thoroughly washes their hands before holding the baby. Smoking around your baby considerably increases the risk of SIDS. Smoking during pregnancy also increases this risk.[7]

CO-SLEEPING

Co-sleeping works for a lot of families all around the world. However, sleeping on the same surface as your baby does carry risks if it isn't handled safely, and you should never fall asleep with your baby on a sofa or chair. (See page 91 for more detail.)

BREASTFEEDING

Breastfeeding for at least two months lowers the risk of SIDS by up to 50%.[8] Combination feeding also reduces the risk.

DUMMIES

Dummies/pacifiers can be in the cot with a baby and pose no risk to them. Some research does actually show that the use of a dummy/pacifier actually reduces the risk of SIDS.[9]

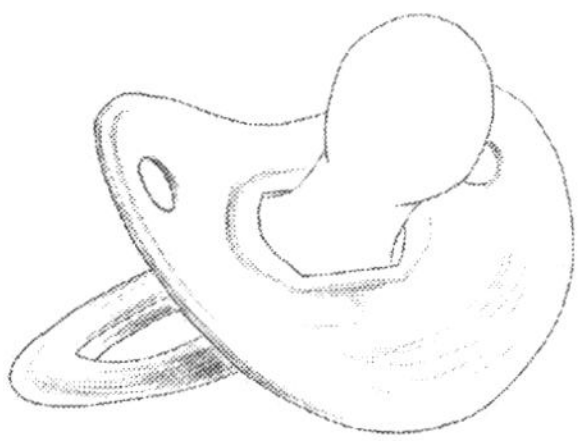

CAR CHAIRS

Car chairs should not be used as a sleep space for a baby as they are not safe to sleep in for long durations. If they are in the car on a journey a baby will often fall asleep but when you have finished the journey, they should be removed from the car chair and placed into a safe sleep space. When babies fall asleep in a sitting position, their heads can fall forward and restrict the airways.

TWINS & MULTIPLES

Ensure that you still practice safe sleep guidelines with twins and multiples. You may find they sleep better in the same cot, so if you decide to do this, ensure that they are either both at one end of the cot (with their feet at the foot of the bed) or at opposite ends (feet to foot). Do not sleep them together in a Moses basket as they may overheat, or rebreathing could be an issue.

POSITIONING THE SLEEP SPACE

Always be mindful where you place the baby's sleep space and ensure that they will be safe wherever they are left to sleep.

HEATING

Never place your baby directly next to a radiator, heater, fireplace, or in direct sunlight. Not only may it overheat the baby, but there is also a risk of burns. For example, if the baby's cot is directly next to a radiator and they put their hand through the cot bars and touch it when hot, they can sustain serious burns. Do not use hot water bottles in the bed when a baby is present.

FANS AND DRAFTS

A fan or open window may be necessary in warmer weather and research has indicated that the use of a fan in rooms that are over 21C may reduce the risk of SIDS. Ensure that any draft from an open window or flow from a fan is not directed at your baby's face constantly. It is important to have air flow within a room, but you don't want to dry your baby's airway out. If your fan has an oscillating option, I would advise this rather than constant flow in one direction.[10]

BLINDS AND CURTAINS

Always ensure that the sleep space is not positioned within reach of blinds or curtains, especially blind cords as if these are not fixed correctly they can be a hazard to your child.

PETS

As much as pets are very much part of our families, there are risks in leaving a baby with a pet unattended, no matter how much you trust your family pet. Babies and children make unpredictable noises, they may pull fur too hard or startle an animal. The best thing you can do is never to allow an animal to share your baby's sleep space or be left in the room unattended with your baby. On a positive note, research does actually show that children who are brought up around family pets (particularly dogs) have a lower risk of asthma.[11]

Cats, in particular, love to sneak into nice cosy spaces. To them, a baby's cot or Moses basket is the perfect place to sleep. To prevent your cat from creeping into the baby's sleep space, have the cot or Moses basket in view before your baby arrives. I guarantee it won't be long before the cat becomes curious and tries to make it their new bed. To prevent this happening and put them off future visits when your baby arrives, put tin foil in the Moses basket/cot. The cat will find it unappealing to lie on, and the foil makes a noise when they tread on it that they dislike. It doesn't take them long to learn that this is not the place to be. When your baby arrives, ensure that your cat does not try and sneak in in the middle of the night. Again, use tin foil, but this time place it on the floor near the sleep space, out of reach of your baby. This should be enough to deter them getting too close.

Animals also carry many germs, and for babies this can be particularly dangerous. You may have the best-groomed pet around, but just remember which areas they lick to clean themselves. I'm sure you wouldn't want them licking your baby after they've done that!

Chapter 2

SLEEP EXPECTATIONS & ADVICE

EXPECTATIONS

When focusing on sleep with babies and young children we have to remember that they all have their own individual characters and needs. When I had twins I realised just how true this is. Maisie and Frankie grew in me at the same time, they received the same nutrients during pregnancy, they experienced the same things as babies, ate the same meals, yet they are very different babies in so many aspects. What works for one of them, when it comes to sleep, doesn't always work for the other. Frankie sleeps very lightly and requires much more comfort if he wakes up during the night. Maisie loves routine and I notice big differences in how bedtime goes if I have rushed through the bedtime routine.

When I was pregnant, my expectation of sleep was that it would be very broken for a long time and I'd have to kiss goodbye to any form of lie in. I was pretty much right about the lie ins. However, what I didn't realise is quite how different my whole life would be. I was no longer working 40+ hours per week, and without work in the first few weeks I actually found that if the night was extremely broken, yes I was tired the next day but I didn't have to do my usual day-to-day job. The stress of work didn't hang over my head and my focus was on the babies. I found that rolling with their rhythm worked so much better than trying to get them to slot into my routine, which would have been nigh on impossible as babies don't know about a nine-to-five work routine. They have no alarm clock telling them when to wake, and their circadian rhythm doesn't start to develop until around 2–4 months of age.[12] They wake in the night because they need something, and they sometimes don't sleep in the day because they either aren't tired enough or have a need that needs tending to before they are able to sleep. If we can accept that babies will slot into our modern day demands when they are developmentally ready, it makes it not so much of a bitter pill to swallow when you are up in the middle of the night for them for the third, fourth or fifth time. Babies do not wake because they want to ruin the following day for you. They wake because they need us. Take pressure off yourself – don't try to get your baby to fit into an adult way of sleep. You will be facing a very hard, uphill battle if you do so.

"80% OF BABIES WAKE UP AT LEAST A COUPLE OF TIMES IN THE NIGHT UP UNTIL THE AGE OF 18 MONTHS. THIS IS NORMAL"

It is one of the first questions that gets asked when you meet someone with your baby – do they sleep well?

People are always quick to tell you if their baby slept through the night from just a few weeks old. But remember, these babies are the minority. In fact, 80% of babies will wake up at least once or twice in the night up until the age of 18 months, and on average once a night until the age of about two years old.[13]

WAKING UP IN THE NIGHT IS NORMAL

Ask your partner or a friend how many times they surface in the night (even before having children!) and I can pretty much guarantee that the answer for most will be once or twice. As adults, we have learnt how to get ourselves back to sleep easily, unlike most babies. Often we don't even remember waking in the night. We may have a bad dream that wakes us, or just stir and fall straight back to sleep. Sometimes we may get out of bed to visit the toilet.

It is human nature to wake for a variety of reasons. The difference with babies is that they cannot see to their needs themselves if they are too cold or hot, hungry, feeling wet, or hearing a noise that startles them. A baby also requires regular feeds due to the size of their stomach. Waking in the night is natural and normal.

UNSOLICITED ADVICE

DEFINITION: NOT ASKED FOR AND POSSIBLY NOT WANTED.
Unsolicited advice is where people (sometimes strangers) give you advice about your baby that you have not asked for. Most of the time this comes from a good place, and people are just trying to help, but the thing with unsolicited advice is it is just that: unsolicited. Also, as the statements are generally based on their personal experience and not on quality evidence surrounding infant sleep, the information offered may be misleading or incorrect. Only you have that intimate knowledge and instincts about your child. Don't get derailed or upset by this sort of advice, however well-meaning.

SLEEP MYTHS

I have heard all sorts of things over the years when it comes to sleep. Nothing surprises me when it comes to old wives' tales. Some even make me laugh out loud. You will struggle to find any hard evidence that backs the following sleep myths up:

Eating solids makes a baby sleep better.

Babies should sleep through the night from six months.

Late bedtime means a later morning wake-up time.

Babies only wake at night because they're hungry.

Reduce the amount of sleep in the day to help them sleep better at night.

Feeding to sleep makes your baby too reliant on you.

Babies can be manipulative to get their way.

Your baby won't learn to self-settle unless you teach them.

Babies don't need night feeds once they're six months old.

Formula-fed babies sleep better.

Weaning early will help your baby sleep better.

Reflux just goes away overnight.

Crying is bad for your baby.

Reading this last one may have made you want to throw this book in the bin! "But she's a gentle sleep consultant," I hear you say. Surely, allowing your baby to cry goes against what this book is all about. That is correct. But I cannot promise you that there will be no tears at any point. What I would never encourage is leaving your baby to cry for an extended period of time alone. As a parent, we learn to understand our baby's various cries. If at any point in this book I talk about allowing your baby to protest a little, I do not mean you should walk out of the room when they are crying with tears. Lots of research has been done about the effects of leaving a baby to cry. You will find some saying it harms, while others conclude that it doesn't.

CRY IT OUT/CONTROLLED CRYING

I feel it is necessary for me to explain my reasons for not advocating various crying methods to get your baby to sleep. These methods come under many different guises, which include:

Cry it out
Controlled crying
Sleep training (note that this doesn't always mean using a cry it out method)
Extinction method
Ferber method

From a personal point of view, listening to a child cry – especially my own child – makes me feel instantly stressed, wanting to do anything in my power to help them. Leaving them untended brings on an anxiety that I feel in the core of my stomach. To me, it only teaches a baby that you aren't coming, and the reason they fall asleep is because they have tired themselves out and given up calling out for you. Over the years I have studied many different areas of psychology and the impact stress has on the body.

So does stress from being left to cry alone cause physical and emotional damage? The evidence isn't clear. Many research papers suggest it doesn't, but on the flip side, plenty show that it does.

One piece of research often brought up to prove that cry it out methods don't cause emotional damage or stress to the baby was a 2016 study of 43 infants, 14 of which received graduated extinction method (left to cry for increasing amounts of time), 15 received bedtime fading technique (adjusting bedtime depending on how tired a baby is) and 14 received sleep education and were the control group. The study found no difference in the stress levels found in the babies.[14]

However, the cortisol levels were tested in the morning and then in the afternoon, not at the actual time of the sleep experiment. The researchers acknowledge that they did not measure acute stress during the time that interventions took place, therefore the actual stress response to being left to cry was unmeasured. The main message that parents are given, when this study is quoted, is that the cry it out method does not cause stress issues for a child.

With crying, there is no clear-cut way of measuring how stressed it makes a baby. For some, it may cause a small amount of stress, yet for others it can be hugely stressful. And with everything else "stressful" that happens in life, how can you measure the scale of impact being left crying had on the baby. If they grow up to have attachment issues, was it because they were left to cry or was it something else that caused it? We'll probably never know.

The decision I've made not to use cry it out methods is based on emotional reasons rather than research results, so much of which is conflicting. I've found that I just cannot leave a child to cry – it doesn't sit well with me. As an adult, if I am upset about something, my husband, friends or family will comfort me. If they just left me to cry, what does that say to me?

Babies do not need to be left to cry for long periods or until they are so tired that they fall asleep. Gentle methods work. Using them carries no risk of stressing your baby out. They work in harmony with your baby and with you.

Those are my personal thoughts though, and parents should be allowed to make their own decisions based on what sits right with them. Do your research if you are considering any of the crying methods.

Of course, if a baby is left to cry when unwell, hungry, or in any danger from an external hazard, this is, in my opinion, neglect.

BUT…

If you or someone else who cares for your child is ever in a situation where they feel overwhelmed to the extent that they fear they may harm a crying baby, it is much safer to leave the baby to cry (provided they are in a safe space and you do not leave them alone in the house). If this happens, seek help from someone immediately. It is better this way than to be in a situation where you or someone else might shake them or do something else that might injure them. If you ever feel you are in a situation where it has all become too much, please seek help from someone. There are many services that can help you and work with you to improve the situation, ensuring everyone is kept safe. See final chapter for helpful services.

Chapter 3

WHAT IS SLEEP?

"A condition of body and mind which typically recurs for several hours every night, in which the nervous system is inactive, the eyes closed, the postural muscles relaxed, and consciousness practically suspended."

We all need sleep. Without sleep we cannot survive.

If you are reading this, I imagine that sleep (or lack of) is impacting your life. It's only when we are deprived of it that we truly realise to what extent it affects our day to day lives. Lack of sleep causes illness, low mood and poor eating habits. But if you are severely sleep deprived for a very long time it can cause obesity, heart disease, high blood pressure and diabetes.[15]

Sleep is a time for our bodies to recover physically, mentally and emotionally. When you're unwell, the best medicine is often sleep. In these hours we also process the day's events and experiences.

Babies sleep a lot. Until the age of two or three, they still sleep in the day also. As newborns, babies sleep most of the time, only waking for short bursts to feed, have a little interaction with their caregiver, and then fall back to sleep.

So much is going on in the first twelve weeks (often called the fourth trimester). This is a period for physical growth, lots of brain development, and adapting to their new world outside the womb. Sleep allows babies time to grow and develop. Although we grow while we are awake, research shows that the majority of growth happens while we sleep.

Humans are born too soon.[16] Some research concludes that humans should not actually be born until 21 months' gestation, but due to the size of our brain and female pelvic outlet, 40 weeks is the most common time for a human baby to be born. The majority of mammals are not so dependent on their parents when born. Most can walk straight away, and fend for themselves to some degree, whereas humans cannot even lift their own heads or sit up! Being attached to you is normal, considering how dependent on its caregiver a baby must be. It is reassuring for your child, and even helps with growth. Lots of skin-to-skin time actually helps with weight gain, particularly for premature babies.[17] It also helps with temperature control, so don't be afraid to hold your baby close. You cannot spoil a baby by holding them too much.

SLEEP STAGES & SLEEP CYCLES

To understand sleep, we need to understand sleep cycles and the stages within a cycle.

All humans go through four stages of sleep, within one sleep cycle, which vary in length depending on age. These four phases make up what is called a sleep cycle. However, the length and presence of these phases vary depending on age.[18]

NREM (NON-RAPID EYE MOVEMENT) STAGE 1

Light sleep

This stage is where you transition from being awake to being asleep. It is a very light phase of sleep and generally lasts 5–10 minutes.

Signs of Stage 1 sleep:
Easily roused. It is very common for a baby to wake from this stage easily. For a while, after being put down in the cot, they are still aware of what is going on around them, even though they may appear asleep.

NREM STAGE 2
Slightly deeper sleep
During this stage, a baby is less likely to be roused easily. It lasts approximately 20 minutes.

Signs of Stage 2 sleep:
Hypnic jerks. This is where the body may jerk (often arms or legs). Body temperature drops slightly and heart rate begins to slow.

NREM STAGE 3
Deep sleep
Not a lot will wake a baby from this very deep phase of sleep. It lasts around 20 minutes.

Signs of Stage 3 sleep:
Muscles relax (if child has a dummy, it may fall out during this phase). Blood pressure and breathing rate drops.

REM (RAPID EYE MOVEMENT) STAGE 4
This is the phase where we dream and the brain becomes more active.

Signs of Stage 4 sleep:
Body is immobilised.
Eyes move rapidly.

A baby up until the age of about 4–6 months (for premature babies' age, see page 46) will generally go through the sleep stage sequence – Stage 2 > Stage 3> Stage 4 – every 40–50 minutes (meaning they drop into a deep sleep fairly quickly).

Around 4–6 months, babies will start to go through Stage 1 (very light sleep) within their sleep cycles, a time where sleep can become interrupted. Often referred to as a regression, it is actually the opposite. The baby is moving towards a more adult-like sleep pattern. The wakes occur because the baby is not used to the light phase of sleep where they are more aware of what is going on around them, even if they appear to be asleep.

SIGNS OF TIREDNESS

Babies display various different signs of being tired and needing to sleep. However, some of the signs actually indicate that they are overtired.

An overtired baby can be very difficult to settle. The key to ensuring your baby is easier to settle is to learn to recognise the difference between early sleep cues and late sleep cues.

EARLY SLEEP CUES

All babies are different and will have different ways of showing you that they are tired. Some of the early sleep cues can be very subtle but you will learn to recognise them once you are aware of them. Some early sleep cues:

Yawning (not within the first 15 minutes of waking)

An obvious sign, yawning is the body's way of trying to take in more oxygen, as when we are tired we don't tend to breathe as deeply. A yawn will give a sudden rush of oxygen to the blood and help expel carbon dioxide. It is our body's way of waking itself up.

Looking pale

Research suggests that when we become tired there are fewer red blood cells flowing in our blood, which can lead to a paler complexion. For babies and children with darker skin tones this may not be as evident, but can be visible inside their mouth where the flesh may appear paler than usual.

Losing interest in what they are doing

Tiredness causes a loss in concentration. A baby may become frustrated carrying out an activity that requires focus or with a toy they're usually happy playing with. They may not seem interested when you read them a book or get distracted and fractious when they are feeding. If your baby is resisting their feed due to loss of concentration, try a feeding necklace. This can be used for both breastfed and bottle-fed babies. The shapes and colours on the necklace will be interesting for them to look at and they can also hold onto it. It gives them something to focus on.

Not wanting eye contact

Gazing away is very common in young babies. Eye contact takes concentration, and when tiredness hits and concentration dwindles, eye contact will be more difficult.

Rubbing their face on you

This can be confused for hunger, so if your baby has been recently fed, this may well be an early tiredness sign.

Pulling at their ears

Ear pulling can be quite common. It is thought that histamine is produced when we become tired, which can cause itchy ears.

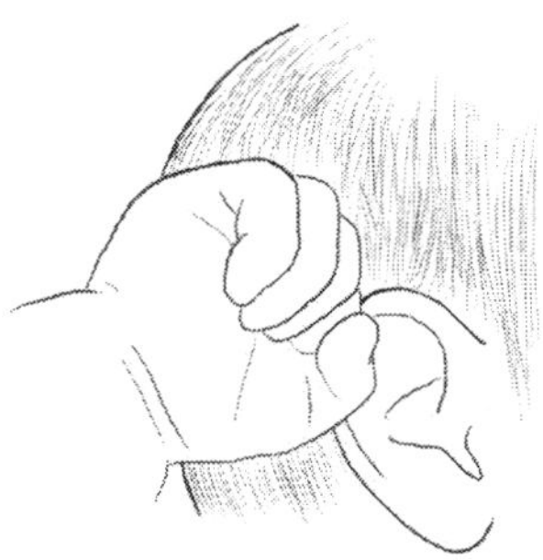

LATE SLEEP CUES

Any of the following late sleep cues are a sign that your baby has become overtired. So when they are displaying them, you should perhaps try getting them down 10–15 minutes earlier than you have been.

Rubbing their face or eyes

Tired eyes get dry, and by rubbing them (or commonly the face in young babies) it helps stimulate the tear ducts to lubricate the eyes. Rubbing the eyes triggers the oculocardiac reflex, which slows the heart rate and makes us feel relaxed.

Crying

Although crying can be a sign of many other things – being hungry, in pain, too hot or cold etc. – it can also signal that a baby is overtired. If they're quick to cry and all their other needs have been met it's most likely. Crying produces the hormone cortisol, which effectively keeps a baby more awake. So next time you see your baby crying from tiredness, take note of how long after their last nap it has taken to get to this point, and try putting them down for a sleep 10–15 minutes before this time in future to avoid tears.

Red eyebrows or frowning

When a baby is overtired, blood rushes to the face, and the redness is most commonly seen around the eyebrow area. This is easier to see on fair-skinned babies. However, if you find that they start frowning or grimacing, this is more often than not a late sleep cue.

Hyperactivity

More common at over eighteen months, if a baby or child becomes hyperactive around sleep times it indicates that they have gone past the point of being tired. Their sleep cues may have been missed or weren't not too obvious. Try to bring the baby or child back to a point where they are calm, and you should find that they settle fairly quickly. Often, hyperactivity is mistakenly taken as a sign that a child is not yet tired, when in fact it is quite the opposite. I speak to so many families who say that their toddler is "full of energy in the evenings". When we work together, we find that, nine times out of ten, the child actually needed a bedtime an hour earlier.

"HYPERACTIVITY IS OFTEN MISTAKEN FOR A CHILD NOT BEING TIRED ENOUGH FOR BED, WHEN, IN ACTUAL FACT, IT IS HIGHLY LIKELY THAT THE EARLY SLEEP CUES WERE MISSED A LONG TIME AGO"

MAXIMUM WAKE TIMES

A maximum wake time is the amount of time a baby can be awake before needing to sleep. For newborn babies this may be only 20–60 minutes before they need to go back to sleep again. Just enough time for a feed and a nappy change.

Over the period of the first few years, this maximum wake time will become longer and longer. At around six months old a baby is likely to be able to stay awake for around two hours before needing to nap again. By the time they are twelve months, this will increase to around three hours, and by the time a child is around three years of age, they are usually able to stay awake all day without a nap. Maximum wake time varies depending on how active a baby is and can be affected by things such as illness, growth spurts and activity levels. Although you should remember that this is just a guide, you might expect maximum wake times to be something like this:

Age	Typical maximum wake time
0–12 weeks	20–60 minutes
3–4 months	1–2 hours
5–7 months	2–2.5 hours
8–12 months	2.5–3.5 hours
12–18 months	3.5–5 hours
18 months–3 years	5–12 hours (12 hours closer to 3 years old)
3 years +	Nap occasionally needed, but may be able to stay awake all day

EXERCISE

This exercise will help you work out your baby's maximum wake time.

To do this you need to make a note of the exact time that they wake up from a sleep and then take note of when they start to show any of the following signs. Ensure that you write down how long this is, as you will notice a pattern.

Carry out this exercise over two consecutive days.

Yawning (not within the first 15 minutes of waking)
Rubbing their face or pulling at their ears
Looking pale
Losing interest in what they are doing
Not wanting eye contact
Rubbing their face on you

After a couple of days writing down this maximum wake time, you will notice a pattern. The times will be very similar, and the average is the maximum wake time. I've included a few tables, as a baby's maximum wake time will vary depending on age, so you may want to do this every couple of months. Sometimes we go with the flow, thinking we know when they are tired, but when we actually focus properly on it, we realise that we are putting them down to sleep too soon or too late, and this turns out to be the root of sleep issues that you are facing.

	Time they woke from sleep	Time they showed early sleep cues	Minutes between wake time and early sleep cues
Day 1			
Day 1			
Day 1			
Day 1			
Day 1			
Day 2			
Day 2			
Day 2			
Day 2			
Day 2			
Day 3			
Day 3			
Day 3			
Day 3			
Day 3			

Day 1 average ______________________________

Day 2 average ______________________________

Day 3 average ______________________________

Average maximum wake time ______________________________

	Time they woke from sleep	Time they showed early sleep cues	Minutes between wake time and early sleep cues
Day 1			
Day 1			
Day 1			
Day 1			
Day 1			
Day 2			
Day 2			
Day 2			
Day 2			
Day 2			
Day 3			
Day 3			
Day 3			
Day 3			
Day 3			

Day 1 average ______________________

Day 2 average ______________________

Day 3 average ______________________

Average maximum wake time ______________________

	Time they woke from sleep	Time they showed early sleep cues	Minutes between wake time and early sleep cues
Day 1			
Day 1			
Day 1			
Day 1			
Day 1			
Day 2			
Day 2			
Day 2			
Day 2			
Day 2			
Day 3			
Day 3			
Day 3			
Day 3			
Day 3			

Day 1 average ______________________________

Day 2 average ______________________________

Day 3 average ______________________________

Average maximum wake time ______________________________

SLEEP LATENCY

Sleep latency means the time it takes to fall asleep. It can tell us a lot about what is going on with a baby's sleep as a whole. It helps determine how much of a sleep deficit your baby may have.

In general, if a baby (not before four months) falls asleep in under 5–10 minutes, it means they are overtired.

An optimum sleep latency is around 15–20 minutes.

Anything over 20 minutes (with resistance) may mean that a baby has severe sleep deprivation, and naps may need adjusting.

EXERCISE

Work out how long your child's average sleep latency is by timing how long it takes for them to fall asleep (from the time you place them down until the time they are asleep). Like the previous exercise, carry this out over 2–3 days. You may notice that their sleep latency becomes shorter as the day goes on.

I have purposefully supplied three exercise charts to fill in, so you can use it at various ages.

	Time placed down to sleep or began to settle them	Time they fell asleep	How many minutes to fall asleep?
Day 1			
Day 1			
Day 1			
Day 1			
Day 2			
Day 2			
Day 2			
Day 2			
Day 3			
Day 3			
Day 3			
Day 3			

Day 1 average ______________________

Day 2 average ______________________

Day 3 average ______________________

Average sleep latency ______________________

Baby age ___________

	Time placed down to sleep or began to settle them	Time they fell asleep	How many minutes to fall asleep?
Day 1			
Day 1			
Day 1			
Day 1			
Day 2			
Day 2			
Day 2			
Day 2			
Day 3			
Day 3			
Day 3			
Day 3			

Day 1 average ______________________

Day 2 average ______________________

Day 3 average ______________________

Average sleep latency ______________________

Baby age ___________

	Time placed down to sleep or began to settle them	Time they fell asleep	How many minutes to fall asleep?
Day 1			
Day 1			
Day 1			
Day 1			
Day 2			
Day 2			
Day 2			
Day 2			
Day 3			
Day 3			
Day 3			
Day 3			

Day 1 average ______________________

Day 2 average ______________________

Day 3 average ______________________

Average sleep latency ______________________

Baby age ___________

Chapter 4

HOW BABIES SLEEP

IN THE WOMB

Babies spend the majority of their time in the womb sleeping. Very little is known about sleep during early fetal development, due to its being unethical to test babies in the womb. Between weeks 38 and 40, it has been found that babies sleep about 95% of the time.[19] However, it is important to note that even in the later stages of pregnancy, if you do feel that there is a change in movements of your baby or you have not felt them move at all, you must get in contact with your midwife or the maternity unit as soon as possible. The majority of the time there will be nothing wrong, but it should not be assumed that your baby is having a sleepy day if their movement pattern differs from what they do normally. Any change in movement is important to get checked. You will NEVER be wasting anyone's time.

Newborn babies will spend most of the time sleeping. When a baby is born, even at 40 weeks' term, their brains are only 30% of the size that they will grow to be, so sleep certainly helps with growth and development.

"IT IS VERY IMPORTANT WHEN FOCUSING ON A PREMATURE BABY'S SLEEP THAT WE USE THEIR CORRECTED AGE"

PREMATURE BABIES & CORRECTED AGE

Babies born before 37 weeks' gestation are classed as premature, and it is very important when focusing on a premature baby's sleep that we use their corrected age. Corrected age is calculated by taking your baby's actual age and subtracting how many weeks premature they were (if born before 37 weeks).

For example, if a baby is born at 35 weeks, when they are 8 weeks old (actual age), their corrected age is 3 weeks old.

Actual age (8 weeks) minus how many weeks early (5) = 3

This is because their brain will develop at the same rate as when it was in the womb. It does not speed up in development once born. Whilst reading through the sleep information in this book, if you have a premature baby please use their corrected age until around 18 months. For babies that are born before 28 weeks (extremely preterm), I would advise using corrected age until they are around 2 years old.

BEFORE 12 WEEKS

Before a baby is about 12–16 weeks old, the pineal gland, which triggers production of melatonin (the sleep hormone) when prompted by darkness, is not developed enough to start melatonin production, meaning that light and dark will make very little difference to how sleepy a baby feels. Before this age, melatonin is present in such a minimal quantity. This does not necessarily mean that you will have a baby that is awake around the clock. In fact, humans fall into a couple of categories – night owl or morning lark.

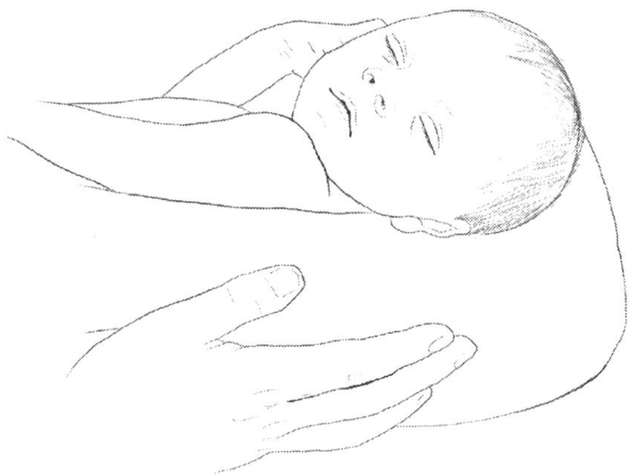

Think of four adults who are close to you. Chances are, a couple of them will be "morning people". These morning larks function well in the early hours, bright and chirpy. And then you have the opposite type of person, who hates getting up early and takes a couple of hours to "warm up" for the day. These night owls function well late at night, often not wanting to go to bed early.

If you think back to caveman days, it makes sense that half of the family unit would be alert late into the night and half alert from the early hours, ensuring that somebody would be awake, no matter what hour it was, to protect the family against danger or predators.

Some babies are naturally night owls, others morning larks. This does not mean that their sleep patterns can't be changed a little, but accepting this as the way they are can make it a little easier.

My husband and I are total opposites when it comes to sleep and it often frustrates me when he cannot get out of bed in the morning, yet I am sure it frustrates him how I cannot stay up much past 10pm. My twins are the same. One of them springs out of bed first thing, while the other will be snuggled under the covers protesting at having to get up. They have had exactly the same food, experiences, and time in the womb together, yet they are so different when it comes to sleep.

Before 12–16 weeks, we can only influence sleep to a very slight degree. As very little melatonin is being produced, there are only a few other influences that will affect sleep – breast milk (formula does not contain any melatonin), temperature, environment, comfort, health, and emotional needs being met.

Research has actually shown that breast milk contains around five times more melatonin at night than during the day, therefore helping a breastfed baby get back to sleep more quickly after a feed at night.[20]

So now that I have gone through the basics of sleep, let's get started.

Chapter 5

INFLUENCES ON SLEEP

ENVIRONMENT

Melatonin (the sleep hormone) is produced when light begins to dim. It should never be underestimated how much the environment a baby sleeps in can affect sleep.

I am a firm believer that we shouldn't have to creep around our own homes while the baby sleeps. Creating an environment that is too quiet can make a child become over-sensitive and unable to sleep through the slightest bit of noise.

That being said, I do believe that the sleep environment should be a calm space and a consistent space, with dimmed lighting. In the first few weeks lighting doesn't matter too much, but once baby is 3+ months, I would encourage darker rooms for daytime naps. It doesn't need to be 100% dark, but the darker the environment, the better quality the sleep. If a baby is in a very light environment for sleep, the optic nerve will sense it and trigger the production of cortisol which is one of the hormones that wake us.[21]

I am not suggesting to sit in a pitch-black room with your baby for daytime sleep, but if you are finding that naps aren't very successful, try reducing the light levels in the room that the baby naps in during the day. Keep the baby away from the light of a TV, as the blue spectrum light interferes greatly with melatonin production.

At six months, where possible, have daytime sleeps in the baby's new room (even if you haven't moved them from your room for nights). This allows for uninterrupted, quality sleep – and means you won't have to sit in a dimly lit room for naps!

LIGHTING (LAMPS/LIGHTBULBS)

Try and have warm-coloured light bulbs in the room where the baby sleeps or winds down. Most lights that you buy for the house are cool white or warm white, so go for the warm white option. Cool lights can give off a bluish tone which can interfere with sleep if you do wind down time in that room.[22]

A great option for night-time feeds or changes is a red lightbulb in a bedside lamp. Red light has very little effect on the suppression of melatonin production, unlike blue light, which is to be found in cool white bulbs, TVs, tablets, phones, and certain brands of plug-ins for colds. Keep these out of sight of a baby when they are in their sleep space.

It may seem extreme, but so many houses have LED bulbs that omit a cool frequency. This can interfere with melatonin production as much as bright sunlight does. Light colour (often referred to as light temperature) is measured on a Kelvin scale.

Light source	Kelvin measurement	Light colour	How much it suppresses melatonin
Daylight (blue sky)	10,000K	Bright sunlight	80% plus
Daylight (overcast)	7,000K	Daytime but overcast	80%
TV/tablet	6,500K	Various	80%
LED bulb (cool white)	6,000K	Bluish, very bright white	80%
LED bulb (warm white)	2,700K	Yellowish, warm white	40%
Filament bulb	2,700K	Soft white	40%
Flickering candle	1,900K	Orange/red	2%
Orange/red light bulb	1,800K	Orange/Red	Less than 2%

You can see from the chart how much melatonin production can be suppressed from various lights and devices. It may not be necessary to change your light bulbs, but it may be a consideration if you have a child that is struggling to fall asleep or wind down in the evening.

Top tip: A simple change from cool white to warm white lighting within the home can make a huge difference to the ambience of a room and also melatonin production for your baby.

"BABIES ARE NOT BORN SCARED OF THE DARK"

FEAR OF THE DARK

Although toddlers may develop an aversion to the dark, this is a learned behaviour and not one they are born with. Dark environments help induce sleep, so night lights which are certain colours are unhelpful to a child's sleep. If you need a small light to use in the middle of the night, ensure it is a red bulb, as this will not interfere with melatonin production as a white bulb might.

DAYLIGHT

Children should be exposed to daylight every day. It has huge benefits, which include:

More vitamin D

In the first week of life, a baby's vitamin D level is dictated by what the mother's levels had been.[23] After this, the sun helps our body to create vitamin D, which is essential for calcium absorption (for healthy bones and teeth). It also helps the immune system.

Exposing a baby as much as possible to daylight when they are not napping is hugely beneficial, so get out of the house whenever possible for some fresh air and bright light. Ensure, however, that your baby is wearing sunscreen if it is a sunny day and that you do not leave them in direct sunlight. If you are unable to leave the house, make sure that curtains or blinds are open, so that light pours in at times when they are not napping.

Better serotonin levels

Serotonin is essential as it helps regulate sleep. It is known as the "happy hormone", so will boost the baby's mood and yours.

Melatonin suppression

Although melatonin production is important, it is also important to have exposure to daylight during the day to ensure that your baby feels sleepy at the right times. You saw from the previous diagram that exposure to daylight suppresses melatonin production by around 80%. If your baby spends all day inside with very little daylight exposure it can cause their circadian rhythm (body clock) to get mixed up.

Managing jaundice

Sunlight helps break down bilirubin, so if you have a baby who is slightly jaundiced (and not requiring hospital treatment for it), 15–30 minutes of sun exposure will be helpful to remove the bilirubin from the bloodstream.[24]

REDUCING LIGHT

My most highly recommended purchase for sleep is a good window covering. Light is the biggest interrupter of sleep, and the main cause of early-waking babies and mixed-up naps. I cannot stress this enough.

Invest in blackout blinds, or if these are too expensive then consider a cheaper solution such as window film (ensure it is compatible with your windows). If light is getting in around the edges of your blackout blinds, think about having curtains over them. Some babies and children are very sensitive to light, and if the optical nerve senses it – it can do this even with eyes closed in a light phase of sleep – it sends a signal to the brain to produce cortisol, which will start the wake-up process. Similar to us drinking a cup of coffee, this waking feeling will be nigh on impossible for the baby or child to fight.

Early wakes during the spring and summer are most often caused by increased light levels in the early hours of the morning that haven't been blocked out sufficiently. Every year I am inundated with parents contacting me as their baby has suddenly started waking early (4/5am). They are often surprised how much difference it can make just blocking out that early morning light.

In the summer months when light still floods into the house around your baby's bedtime, consider shutting curtains to block out light about an hour before bedtime and having dimmed lighting.

SOUND

General household noise cannot be avoided, and, as mentioned before, I wouldn't recommend actively trying to reduce household noise as your baby will adapt to the sounds within your home, such as other children, a dog barking, the hoover, and voices. However, some children are very noise sensitive and can be roused easily by the slightest sound.

Using a device that emits white noise or pink noise during sleep times can be a great tool to help drown out some of the sounds that may otherwise interrupt their sleep. White noise sounds very much like a hissing, or the sound of static. Pink noise is quite a new concept when it comes to aiding sleep and, although very similar to white noise, it has a slightly different sound which can mask low-frequency background noise. Smoother and more soothing, some research shows that pink noise has a better effect on sleep and can help induce deeper sleep.[25]

Using sound as a sleep aid very rarely causes long-term reliance. It can be used without the parent present, and there are lots of great apps available online that will play white/pink noise continually for twelve hours or more, if needed. If you feel this is something that you don't want playing continually, switch it off once your baby is in a deep sleep (when muscles have relaxed and breathing has slowed).

If you want to phase the use of it out, gently do so over a two-week period by reducing the volume every couple of days.

Music

Soothing songs or lullabies can be used as an effective sleep association. Classical music and lullabies, particularly in preterm babies or babies in NICU, have shown to reduce stress, maintain body temperature and increase oxygen levels.[26]

Babies, even as young as three months, can pick out the complex structure of classical music and even recognise music that has been played to them before.

Singing to your baby helps them learn language. Never underestimate how much a baby soaks up. You don't need to be an amazing singer either, your baby will be soothed by your familiar voice.[27]

Music is also a very positive sleep association as it can be played even when you are not present in the room.

MILK FEEDING

Sometimes sleeping issues are actually feeding issues in disguise. Feeding helps regulate a baby's circadian rhythm, particularly in breastfed babies.

Whichever way you choose to feed, ensure that it is your choice and not influenced by other people's stories about how it affected their babies' sleep. There is very little difference in how a breastfed baby or formula-fed baby sleeps.

A breastfed baby may feed more frequently than a formula-fed baby, due to the breast milk being broken down more quickly than formula, meaning a baby may become hungry sooner. Breastfed babies are also not fed on a schedule, so will feed when they are hungry rather than having the more structured feed times typical with formula-fed babies.

Regular feeding is natural and very normal. Often a breastfed baby will go through stages of "cluster feeding", whilst going through a growth spurt, when they may feed on and off for long durations. This frequent feeding helps to increase the milk supply needed for the growth spurt. These phases usually last a few days before settling down again.

That being said, breastfeeding a baby doesn't require you to have to physically get up, leave the room and make a bottle up. When breastfeeding, a lot of mothers don't even remember how many times a child wakes in the night, as the baby is generally right next to them. They give them a feed and go straight back to sleep. There are some fantastic cots that sit at the same level as the adult bed, meaning you can very easily bring your baby to you for a feed (or they come to you when mobile) without your having to get out of bed.

Breastfeeding is also very much about comfort. Often, the feeling of being close to their mother, skin to skin and latching on (even if only for a few moments), can be enough to settle a baby back to sleep. You are your baby's best sleep aid!

A breastfed baby will get the perfect amount of milk from their mother at each feed. Some feeds may be longer, some shorter, but you shouldn't need to worry that your baby isn't getting enough as breast milk works on a supply and demand basis. A woman's body will produce more if a baby feeds more often or for longer and will also adjust as feeds become less frequent. If ever in doubt about breastfeeding, the best person to speak to is an IBCLC (lactation consultant) as they will be able to give you the best possible information and advice. Many doctors, health visitors and even midwives do not go through a huge amount of training when it comes to feeding infants so a lactation consultant will certainly be able to offer you a wealth of knowledge. They go through a minimum of 90 hours of education for anything up to a five-year period, unlike many other health professionals who may only have had a few days' or even hours' training.

Remember that how you feed your baby is your choice, but it is important to make an informed one, and not one based on other people's experiences. Remember, no two journeys are the same when it comes to breastfeeding. If this is not your first child and you chose not to breastfeed last time, or found that you couldn't, it doesn't mean that you can't try breastfeeding this time. Find yourself good breastfeeding support. This can be invaluable.

There may be various reasons why you choose to formula feed your baby. Let it be your choice and not influenced by others. Formula feeding or bottle feeding your baby with expressed breast milk allows others to feed your baby too. This can be a fantastic bonding time for your partner with the baby, and takes the pressure off the mother being the sole feeder, allowing a little more freedom if she has other commitments and cannot be around for every feed. A lot of parents who choose to bottle feed their baby will also share night-time feeds, allowing both parents to have more consolidated sleep.

If you decide to formula feed your baby, there are so many options out there when it comes to choosing what brand to go with or which bottles to choose. All first infant milk has a guaranteed nutritional composition. The majority of first infant milks will be so similar in ingredients that it does not matter whether you use one that is the cheapest or the most expensive: they will still contain a minimum amount of protein, vitamins and nutrients. There's a great number of formula types available (see table). Always use first infant milk for the first six months, unless advised by a doctor otherwise.

Formula type	Benefits	For ages	Points to note
First Infant Milk	Unless a health professional suggests otherwise, first infant formula is the only formula your baby needs. It will contain the required vitamins, minerals and nutrients	From birth	All first infant milks on the UK market must meet compositional regulations. Ingredients will only vary slightly by brand. Just because a brand is more expensive, it does not necessarily mean that it is better for your baby
Follow-on Milk	Contains slightly different vitamin and mineral content to first infant milk	From 6 months	Unnecessary to change to as additional vitamins and nutrients can be found in food
Comfort Milk	May help ease colic-like symptoms or digestive discomfort	Under direction from a doctor or health professional	Contains partially hydrolysed proteins that are easier to digest. Not usually beneficial for babies with reflux
Hungry Baby Milk	May keep baby fuller for longer due to protein differences	Under direction from a doctor or health professional	Can cause constipation which can cause greater issues.
Anti-Reflux Milk	Can help milk stay down for babies suffering with reflux	Under direction from a doctor or health professional	Can cause constipation and may be unnecessary if baby is gaining weight on first infant milk

Formula type	Benefits	For ages	Points to note
Dairy-free Formula	Suitable for babies suffering with a CMPA (cow's milk protein allergy)	Under direction from a doctor or health professional	Unnecessary if baby doesn't have a diagnosed CMPA
Weight Gain Formula	Suitable for babies born prematurely and failing to gain weight or for babies with malabsorption-related conditions	Under direction from a doctor or health professional	Unnecessary unless prescribed by a doctor
Lactose-free Milk	Suitable for babies with a lactose intolerance	Under direction from a doctor or health professional	Unnecessary unless prescribed by a doctor
Goat's Milk Formula	Less allergenic and less lactose than cow's milk based formulas. Easier digestion.	From 6 months unless under direction from a doctor	An alternative to first infant milk after 6 months.
Toddler Milk	Wide range of vitamins included	From 12 months	An alternative to cow's milk from 12 months, however is not necessary

When bottle feeding a baby, ensure that they are well winded after all feeds. Unlike breastfed babies, who suffer far less with wind issues, it is imperative that time is spent winding your baby after all feeds, even in the night. This can be done gently without waking them too much by using more of a rubbing motion on their back than a patting motion. I find that using various winding methods rather than one method constantly is very effective.

Here are a few of my favourite methods.

Over the shoulder

Probably one of the most traditional winding positions. Hold your baby with their front against yours and their chin over your shoulder so they are looking behind you. Support their bottom but let their legs hang free and gently rub or pat their back. Keep their back as straight as possible as this will help the wind come up. Keep doing this until it happens. Swap positions to another winding technique after you have done this for a minute or so if no wind has come up.

Seated

Sit down and put your baby in a sitting position on your lap so that they are facing away from you, sitting to the side. Ensure their feet are hanging free so they are not touching a floor or anything that supports their feet. It is really important that they hang free. Keep their back as straight as possible. Imagine that they have a corset on so the spine is all in line and support their head with your hand under their chin. Rub or pat your baby's back until the wind comes up.

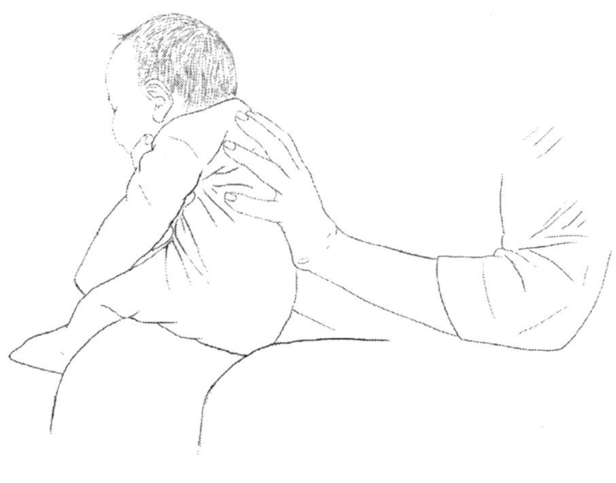

Tummy winding

Lay your baby on their tummy over your lap. It is very important that you support their head. This position is often useful to do for 20–30 seconds to break up the other techniques, so you could do over the shoulder winding for a few minutes then tummy winding and then back to over the shoulder. A lot of babies don't like the tummy winding position as it can feel a little strange for them. Be careful that this position is only used for a very short time if they have a full tummy.

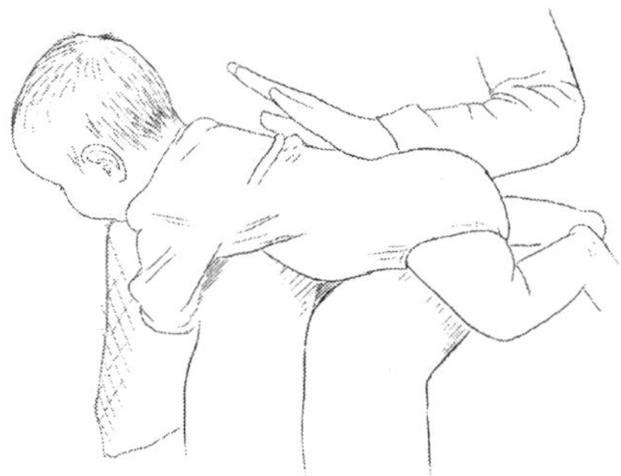

Stand to attention

Holding your baby so they face away from you, hold them in a vertical position with their back against your tummy and their legs hanging free. Keep their back as straight as possible. If your baby does not have head control, ensure their head doesn't fall forward. Stand up when doing this with your baby and just stand still. The straighter their back is, the better. You may need to stand like this for a few minutes but it is a great position to use if you do not want to wake a baby too much after a night feed. This position can cause wind to go down rather than up a lot of the time!

FOOD

FOODS FOR SLEEP

Certain foods have shown to help sleep. Here are a few examples.

Rice (particularly jasmine rice)

Lean meats such as turkey and chicken

Fish such as salmon, tuna and halibut – rich in Vitamin B6 which the body needs to make serotonin and melatonin

Cheese, milk and yoghurts (rich in calcium which helps aid sleep)

Walnuts and almonds (ground up into meals or in the form of a nut butter)

Cherries (particularly tart cherries) contain melatonin. Must be prepared correctly so don't serve whole as they pose as a choke hazard.

Kiwi fruit – high in serotonin.

Green leafy vegetables

Oats – a great natural source of melatonin

FOODS THAT MAY HINDER SLEEP

Certain foods may cause sleep disturbances due to overstimulation of the gut or digestive discomfort. Foods should be introduced gradually to babies and children, to ensure that no allergy is present or that they don't find the food difficult to tolerate.

"BROCCOLI AND CAULIFLOWER CAN BE VERY HARD TO DIGEST"

Caffeine – fairly obvious as caffeine is a stimulant, but be aware that it is present in lots of things – not just tea and coffee – like chocolate, and chocolate-flavoured foods such as breakfast cereals, chocolate drinks or chocolate ice cream. It is also present in lots of fizzy drinks

Spicy foods can increase body temperature meaning it may be more difficult to fall asleep.

Red meats – high in protein which takes longer to break down, making it harder to drop off to sleep and can cause digestive discomfort.

Broccoli and cauliflower – if eaten too close to bedtime, broccoli and cauliflower can be slow to digest, preventing a child from falling asleep. Try having this closer to lunchtime than bedtime as it is a great source of nutrition but may hinder night-time sleep.

Tomatoes – a great source of nutrition, but they can be quite acidic and cause digestive discomfort if given in large quantities. Avoid this at later meals of the day (particularly for babies who have acid reflux).

ALLERGIES

It is often hard to ascertain if a baby is having sleep issues due to certain foods, as diets can be so varied and containing multiple ingredients. It is always best to introduce different foods one at a time and allow three days before introducing a new food to ensure that if an allergy or intolerance is suspected you can easily work out what is causing allergic reaction or the sleep disturbance.

Intolerances are far more common than actual allergies, and most babies grow out of mild to moderate intolerances by about 12–18 months.

If you have a baby who is regularly waking throughout the night after weaning and wasn't before, it is worth filling in a food diary for 2–3 weeks as this will help you identify if a certain food is causing disturbance and then it can be omitted or reduced in quantity.

FOOD DIARY

Using the table on page 66 list the foods eaten at any meal, including breaking down pre-made food into ingredients. With these, ingredients are listed on the label in order of quantity of ingredient in the food. For example, if an ingredients list reads: vegetable stock, onions, tomatoes, potatoes, butternut squash, chicken, mangoes, organic spices, then this means the vegetable stock is present in the highest percentage and the organic spices the smallest.

If you are formula feeding a baby and they are exclusively on a milk diet, be aware that some milks will contain different ingredients to others. Although all first infant milks have to have a minimum nutritional content, ingredients do vary. As an example, some milk contains fish oil and some does not. The ingredients that are most likely to cause an allergy or intolerance are always highlighted in **bold** on ingredients lists.

If your baby is allergic to an ingredient, symptoms may include:

Diarrhoea or vomiting
A cough after eating the food/milk
Wheezing or shortness of breath*
Itchy throat or tongue
Itchy skin or rash
Swollen lips or throat*

Runny or blocked nose after eating the food/milk
Sore, red or itchy eyes
Mucus in stools

If your baby displays any of these symptoms then consult with your doctor. Don't remove first infant milk from their diet and substitute for an alternative that may be free from dairy unless directed by your doctor.

*** If your baby has trouble breathing or their lips, tongue or throat swell, seek emergency medical assistance immediately.**

Foods that most commonly cause an allergic reaction (generally highlighted in bold on ingredients lists) are:

Cow's milk
Eggs
Foods that contain gluten including barley, wheat and rye
Nuts and peanuts (serve crushed, never whole)
Seeds (serve crushed not whole)
Soya
Shellfish (must be completely cooked, never raw or partially cooked)
Fish

These foods can be introduced from around six months (cow's milk at 12 months but is OK if used in cooking or small quantities in meals).

Evidence has shown that delaying the introduction of peanuts and eggs beyond 6–12 months may increase the risk of developing an allergy to these foods.[29]

Most babies will grow out of allergies to the foods listed, however a peanut allergy is generally lifelong. Most doctors will be able to guide you on allergies or refer you to a specialist if required.

Always read food labels very carefully. If a food label is unavailable and you are unsure of the ingredients in the food (for example if you are eating at a friend's house and they don't know exactly what was in all sauces etc.) then avoid them if you have a child who has a known allergy.

Intolerance is different to an actual allergy and will generally cause less severe symptoms than an allergy, which could be life threatening. For example, red meat can be difficult to digest and cause discomfort for your child, but this does NOT mean they are allergic to it – more that they struggle to digest it well.

Skin allergies caused by food are quite common in babies and young children, mainly in food that is acidic such as tomatoes, citrus fruits and spices. If you feed your baby a food and they get a rash on their face where it has touched it, ensure you wipe it away as quickly as possible. Speak to your doctor if this happens to get their professional opinion as to whether it is something you should omit from their diet.

A resistance to sleep caused by food discomfort can include symptoms such as back arching, thrashing arms, red face, increased passing of wind, and clenched fists.

Keeping a food diary can help you rule out anything which may be causing sleep interruptions.

Again, do not omit milk unless advised by your doctor, as milk is a baby's main source of nutrition.

If you are breastfeeding your baby, keep a food diary too so that you can see if anything you are eating or drinking is affecting their sleep or causing discomfort. A baby that has a cow's milk protein allergy (CMPA) may show signs of discomfort when the mother has eaten lots of dairy, for example. If you do have a baby with a cow's milk protein allergy and you are breastfeeding, omit dairy from your diet. NICE guidelines (National Institute for Clinical Excellence) advise that you carry on breastfeeding while you remove dairy. There should be no need to use formula in the meantime, and you usually see a difference in a few days, even though it can take 2–3 weeks for the milk proteins to completely leave your body.

If the mother is having excessive caffeine (about 2–3 cups of coffee is safe for breastfeeding mothers to consume per day) some babies will be sensitive to the caffeine. It may increase alertness. As previously mentioned, caffeine isn't just found in tea or coffee, it is in other things too, such as chocolate. (Sorry!)

Most over-the-counter medications are safe to take whilst breastfeeding, but some medications are unsafe to use while doing so. Always check on the packet that they are safe for breastfeeding mothers and let your GP know that you are breastfeeding if you are being prescribed medication.

The use of antibiotics does not generally necessitate suspension of breastfeeding.[30] The Breast Feeding Network has a very comprehensive guide on medications and breastfeeding.[32]

FOOD DIARY

Day	Food eaten	Resistance to sleep? Y/N	Increased gas? Y/N	Skin rash? Y/N
1				
1				
1				
1				
1				
2				
2				
2				
2				
2				
3				
3				
3				
3				
3				

COLIC & REFLUX

Colic is a symptom of an underlying issue. The NHS defines colic as continual crying for more than three hours for a minimum of three days a week for over a week. You may also see symptoms such as clenching of fists, bringing their knees up to their tummy, and going very red in the face. They will most likely be very difficult to settle.

Signs of possible reflux include:

- Milk or food visibly coming up into the mouth and often spilling out of the mouth
- Lots of swallowing or gulping after a feed or when being winded (an attempt to swallow down the rising milk/feed)

- Coughing or hiccuping while feeding or shortly after
- Being unsettled during a feed
- Becoming very unsettled when laid down horizontally.
- Short naps of 20–30 minutes (consistently) after a feed and waking up very distressed

I often recommend doing a "tablespoon test" to parents that are concerned with the amount of milk that comes up (in a baby that is gaining weight). It demonstrates how a small volume of milk can actually make a huge mess and cause worry.

A tablespoon is about 15ml (approximately half an ounce).

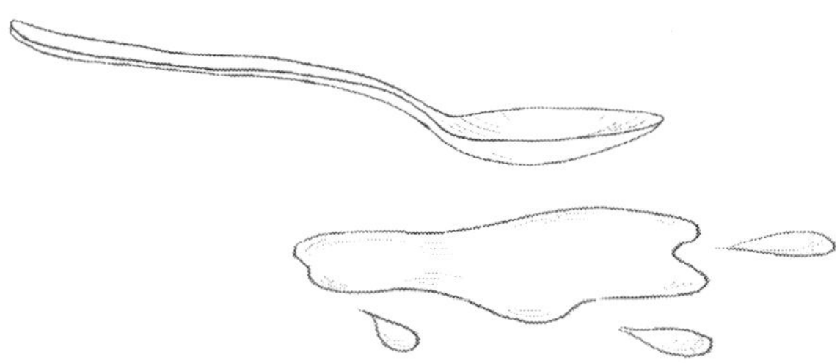

Fill a tablespoon with ordinary milk (not baby milk) and then pour this onto your kitchen worktop. You will see how much mess it makes. If your baby is bringing up that amount or less, still gaining weight, and producing 6–8 wet nappies a day, it shouldn't be a cause for worry, just more laundry! They will grow out of this gradually as they gain better head control and start sitting upright more.

Generally, once a baby starts on more solid food, at around six months, the reflux will lessen as food has a thicker consistency and stays down better. A baby who suffers with reflux will generally grow out of it around 12–18 months.

Be aware that when they have food, although it may not come up into their mouth due to it being thicker, it may still rise up the throat with stomach acid and cause a bit of discomfort. Feed your baby slowly to allow the food time to go down and avoid laying them flat directly after a meal.

Very often, issues such as trapped wind, an intolerance/allergy, GOR (gastro oesophageal reflux), or GORD (gastro oesophageal reflux disease, sometimes referred to as GERD) can be the cause of colic. GOR is physiological and is often seen in babies of low birth weight or premature babies, though this is by no means the only cause and it can actually be seen in around 40% of babies.[31] The primary cause is that the lower oesophageal sphincter (muscles at the bottom of the oesophagus and top of the stomach) is not fully developed. Therefore, instead of holding a feed down, because the valve is weak it will let amounts of the feed out. Often this is when the baby is horizontal, meaning the valve opens more easily, or if the baby is winded vigorously (patted not rubbed) or moved around straight after a feed. This is generally a laundry issue, with only small amounts of feed coming up, and it does not affect the growth of the baby.

The key thing is to ensure that the baby is gaining weight and also that the nappy output is normal (6–8 wet nappies in 24 hours). A baby that suffers from GOR and still gains weight may still suffer from discomfort that interrupts sleep.

GORD, however, can be a sign of an underlying issue. The oesophagus could be damaged from the reflux, the reflux is often projectile, and the baby gains little or no weight.[28] If they are producing fewer than 6–8 wet nappies in 24 hours this may be a sign of dehydration. If the baby is in this situation, seek medical advice from your doctor as soon as possible.

There are a few things you can do to help a baby whose reflux is disrupting sleep:

- If bottle feeding, hold your baby in a more upright position
- Wind halfway through a feed, and thoroughly afterwards
- Rub their back, don't pat it to bring wind up or hold in the "stand to attention" winding position
- Tilt your baby slightly to the left when feeding them (breastfed or bottle-fed babies)
- Try and hold them as upright as possible for 20–30 minutes after a feed. They do not need to be completely upright, so you could place them in an angled baby chair if you cannot hold them this length of time or in a sling, which is very effective.
- Avoid tummy time directly after feeding
- When making formula bottles up, swirl the formula instead of shaking it, as shaking will put more air bubbles in the liquid

Although elevating a cot is often recommended, research does show that it makes very little difference, if any. Elevating a cot too much at one end may cause a baby to move too far down it, and possibly under any covers or into an awkward position. If you want to elevate the cot, only do so very slightly. The cot should still be empty. Wedges designed to help reflux have not been proven safe within a cot.[33]

If you still find that your baby is bringing up a lot of milk, speak to your GP if you feel it is causing weight gain issues or causing discomfort. There are products available, which can even be used for breastfed babies, that will thicken the milk in the stomach. Some of these thickening products are natural, such as carob gum. A breastfed baby can have this neat before a feed, and for a formula-fed baby it can be added to the milk. Always consult with your doctor before using any thickening products.

NEVER add cereal to a bottle to thicken milk as it is a choking hazard.

There are anti-reflux milks available on the market, but seek guidance from a health professional before starting on these as they can cause constipation.

Comfort milks are talked about a lot too, but are often different in consistency to first infant milk and not necessarily beneficial for babies with reflux.

As a parent of a reflux baby myself, I do not want to downplay how hard it can be, and sometimes quite distressing, but be reassured that it is fairly common and they do grow out of it. Have plenty of bibs or muslins available at feed times, take feeds slowly, and always wind them thoroughly during and after a feed.

Reflux doesn't usually just go away overnight – it is more of a gradual process. It is mainly a physiological issue, and should become less severe as the baby grows. As mentioned before, lots of people assume it goes away when solids are started, but it may still be present and cause symptoms.

Silent reflux is where you do not see anything come up into the mouth but it may still be rising up the oesophagus, causing discomfort.

Tongue/lip tie and reflux

It may be worth having tongue/lip tie ruled out by an IBCLC if your baby suffers with reflux. A poor latch caused by either of these can mean too much air is taken in when feeding. A study in 2016 showed significant improvements in a baby's reflux once a frenotomy procedure had taken place (to release the tongue or lip tie).[34] Tongue tie is thought to affect between 4 and 11% of babies.

Craniosacral therapy
Craniosacral therapy (cranial osteopathy) is a gentle therapy carried out by an osteopath that works with the body using light touch. It helps the neck and diaphragm of the baby relax, which in turn can make feeding more efficient, and has been shown to alleviate reflux in some cases.

ANXIETY

Becoming a parent is an anxious time, and nothing heightens anxiety more than sleep deprivation.

Have you ever had a situation where you cannot settle your baby for love nor money, then a friend comes round and holds the baby, which immediately quietens? This is in no way a sign that your friend is "better with babies" or that the baby is unhappy with you. Remember, that friend is not living your life 24/7.

Babies sense emotions. If a situation gets too much, it is OK to step away for a few moments (so long as your baby is safe), take a deep breath, then go back to the situation again.

Know that phases of crying consistently, not being able to settle, or not being able to comfort your child are phases that usually only last a few minutes, yet can seem like a lifetime when you are in the thick of it. There is no harm in asking your partner or a friend/family member if they can try and settle your baby so that you can take five minutes to get yourself together. You will be surprised, once you have regrouped and relaxed a little, how much more effective you will be at settling your child back down to sleep.

TAKE THE PRESSURE OFF YOURSELF – YOU ARE NOT SUPERHUMAN

TEETHING

Teething can affect feeding and also cause very frequent waking.

If your baby is suffering with teething pain, put teething gel on 10–15 minutes before a milk feed. This may soothe their gums so that when they have a feed it is more comfortable for them.

Please note that some teething gels and granules contain food-grade lactose which should be avoided for children with CMPA due to the risk of cow's milk protein contamination.

When a baby is teething, if they feel pain they will wake. The key thing is to manage their pain with either teething toys, gel, granules or liquids.

If you know that they are suffering with teething and a tooth is about to break through, and if other teething aids have not helped, it may be beneficial to use a pain reliever such as infant paracetamol or ibuprofen. Follow dosage instructions as advised on the product.

The next diagram shows you which teeth may be causing the pain at certain times. You can then apply teething gel, liquid or granules on the area where the tooth is breaking through, rather than all over the mouth.

Teething rattles/rings are very helpful during the day, as a baby can bite down on them to help ease discomfort.

PRIMARY TEETH

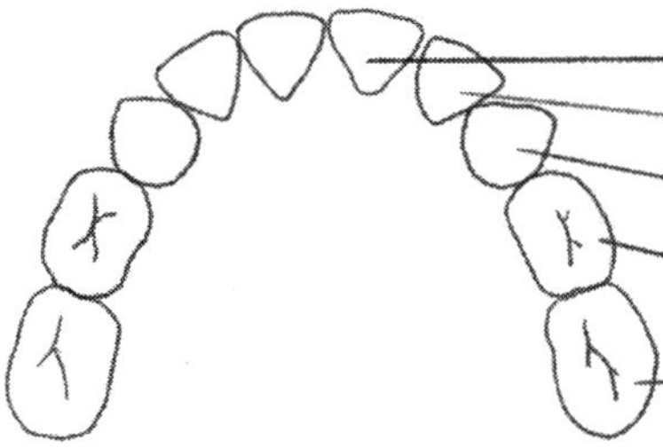

UPPER TEETH	ERUPT	SHED
Central incisor	8–12 months	6–7 years
Lateral incisor	9–13 months	7–8 years
Canine (cuspid)	16–22 months	10–12 years
First molar	13–19 months	9–11 years
Second molar	25–33 months	10–12 years

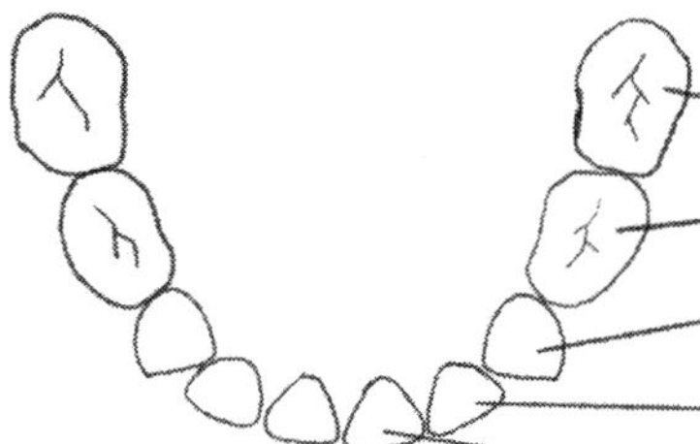

LOWER TEETH	ERUPT	SHED
Second molar	25–31 months	10–12 years
First molar	14–18 months	9–11 years
Canine (cuspid)	17–23 months	9–12 years
Lateral incisor	10–16 months	7–8 years
Central incisor	6–10 months	6–7 years

Top tip: when using a new teething gel, granules or liquid products, try a small amount on your gums first. Some products have very strong taste and often "less is more". You do not want to upset your baby further by putting too much of a strong-tasting product on. Some products contain numbing agents as well, which can be a strange sensation, especially if it gets on the tongue if too much is applied.

Chapter 6

GETTING PREPARED FOR SLEEP

PREPARING FOR YOUR NEW ARRIVAL

"IF YOU THINK YOU'RE TIRED NOW, WAIT UNTIL THEY ARRIVE"

How many times did you hear that from somebody whilst you were pregnant? Annoying isn't it? Unsolicited advice and unwanted comments many expectant parents have to put up with.

However, no two babies are the same, and no two pregnancies are either.

As a parent of twins I can tell you that I actually got more better quality sleep (even though I got less sleep) once the babies had arrived, due to having been so uncomfortable during pregnancy. Of course this is not the case for everyone, but certainly the later stages of pregnancy can be full of very broken sleep.

During pregnancy I was constantly going to the toilet in the night, only able to lie on my left side (the safest side to lie on whilst pregnant) and generally feeling so uncomfortable. This is definitely not just the case in a twin or multiple pregnancy either, far from it. When pregnant, you may be in bed for an average of 8–10 hours at night, but in the later stages of pregnancy how many of those are you actually fast asleep with no physical discomfort? Not 8–10, unless you are one of the very lucky minority. A lot of women are unable to sleep lying down completely flat towards the end of their pregnancy due to discomfort. I can promise you that once your baby arrives, you will be able to lie flat in your own bed at least!

"THE FIRST FEW WEEKS AFTER YOUR BABY ARRIVES IS TIME FOR YOU TO ADJUST, RECUPERATE AFTER BIRTH AND GET TO KNOW YOUR NEW ADDITION."

Often during pregnancy we have the stress of work the next day, which can be physically and mentally exhausting. When your baby arrives, the focus is on them and yourself. If you have taken maternity leave, you no longer have the stress of work hanging over you, and it is up to you how many commitments you make the next day.

Don't feel pressured to commit to numerous meet-ups if you don't feel ready. Staying in your pyjamas all day is absolutely fine, especially with a newborn. The first few weeks after your baby arrives is time for you to adjust, recuperate after birth and get to know your new addition, and for them to get to know you.

Lots of people will advise "sleep when they sleep", which isn't always practical. But if you can do it, then do it, and don't feel guilty!

Your sleep will be different. At times it will be testing on you, but if you can learn your baby's sleep needs it will enable you to predict when you can have some rest time too.

THE FIRST TWO WEEKS

Your baby will generally spend the first couple of weeks after birth simply feeding and sleeping, and usually sleeping fairly soundly. It is a time where most parents say that they have a dream sleeper. However, and not to be negative, this stage is generally short-lived. After the two weeks, they start to be more alert and have a need for more stimulation.

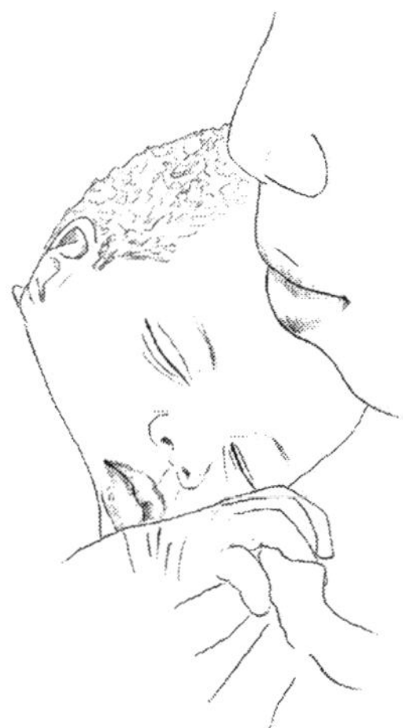

During the first few days, your body will be adjusting to the huge changes of hormones. Directly after birth, oxytocin (the happy hormone) and prolactin (which encourages milk production) increase, and progesterone and oestrogen decrease. You may find that, after a few days, the oxytocin reduces, and it is then common to feel "baby blues". You may be teary, stressed or anxious, but be reassured that, over the next week or two, these hormones will usually settle. If these feelings don't seem to lift after a few weeks, do speak with a health professional. Feeling overwhelmed is nothing to be ashamed about. Some women suffer from postnatal depression after birth, but if it goes untreated it can last for many months. Men can also suffer from depression after birth, so it is important to be aware of this as help is available for both parents. I cover postnatal mental health, more in depth, in Chapter 12.

The first two weeks is the perfect time to recuperate, as babies are usually fairly calm for this period. My recommendation would be to minimise visitors, certainly for the first 2–3 days, and have family time with your new addition. This is not the time to be having to make drinks for visitors, or feel that you need to make yourself look presentable. This is a time for adjustment, where lazing around all day between your bed and the sofa is actually a good idea. Don't get me wrong, keep mobile and get some fresh air, but don't feel guilty about being in your pyjamas all day. You may need the recovery time.

If visitors do come, ask them to bring meals that can be heated up easily instead of flowers. You have a new baby to look after and, as nice as twenty bunches of flowers are, you don't need to be feeding and watering twenty other things a day in addition to your baby.

Spend these two weeks having plenty of skin-to-skin time with your baby. If you are breastfeeding, this will help with establishing your milk supply.

Skin to skin has so many other benefits, such as helping to regulate your baby's body temperature and having a calming effect on both you and your baby as it helps release oxytocin (the happy hormone). Spend this time soaking up every second of this time with your new baby (or babies!)

You will find that in not having commitments, and not being worried about people coming round while the baby is feeding or sleeping, it will give you a great start.

That being said, I am sure lots of friends and family will want to visit, but try not to pass the baby round too much. If your baby is only putting on weight very slowly or has lost too much weight shortly after birth, try to have as little overstimulation as possible. If the baby becomes overstimulated it will of course burn more calories, and this doesn't help with weight gain.

You will find that your baby naps on and off around the clock, generally to a routine of feed, sleep, wake, feed, sleep, wake etc. The wakeful periods will likely be very short (20–40 minutes).

Premature babies (born before 37 weeks) will probably follow this pattern until they are a month or so past their due date.

In the first couple of weeks, you shouldn't let your baby sleep for more than four hours without a feed. Although breastfeeding is on demand and not scheduled, if your baby is sleeping for more than four hours you should try and get them to feed from you. If your baby is gaining weight and producing 6–8 wet nappies a day, this is a sign that they are getting what they need. If your baby is constantly drowsy, having very few periods of being awake, and not feeding well, consult your healthcare professional. If they are producing fewer than six wet nappies in a 24-hour period, speak to your doctor, as this may indicate that they are not feeding sufficiently and becoming dehydrated.

Remember that your baby does not know the difference between night and day at this age, so you may find that they are more alert at night. This does not mean that it is a sign of things to come. It will adjust as your baby's brain develops and melatonin starts being produced at around 12–16 weeks (corrected age).

Even though your baby is sleeping so much, you can start from birth to introduce positive sleep associations and a little bit of a bedtime/wake up routine.

WAKE UP ROUTINE

Begin by starting your day at the same time every day. Aim between 6 and 8am for this. Let some light into the room and change your baby's nappy. If you are bottle feeding, you would offer the first feed of the day at this time, and have this feed at the same time every day, where possible, if you want to start a bit of structure to your day.

If you are breastfeeding, you may have fed very recently, but it is a good time to offer the breast to your baby as the hormone cortisol is three times higher in the morning than in the evening milk. Research has shown that breast milk has different compositions of hormones depending on the time of day, so milk that is expressed in the early evening was found to have higher levels of melatonin.[35] Breast milk is so clever, adapting itself according to demand, time of day, if a baby is unwell, or even when the mother is unwell. You will find antibodies in breast milk to prevent the baby getting sick when the mother is. The human body is amazing!

Once your baby has been fed, wind your baby, and then if they are drowsy pop them back to sleep (and you go back to sleep if you need to). If awake and alert, get up for the day with them. Ensure the room is light when they are awake. If this morning routine doesn't work for you in the first few weeks, don't stress, just focus on the bedtime routine. It is often much more enjoyable in the evening as we are feeling much more awake!

BEDTIME ROUTINE

Introduce a sequence of events in the evening before bedtime. In the first few weeks I wouldn't recommend bath-time being part of this routine every night. A young babies' skin is very delicate so a bath isn't advised every night, but you can give them a wash down with cotton wool and water and this can still be relaxing for them.

Consider massage and a lullaby, dimmed lights and quiet voices before you settle them down for the evening. Skin to skin time will also be beneficial to regulate their body temperature and reassure them. The key thing in the first couple of weeks is not to over stimulate a baby before bed. Over stimulating can happen in many different ways, such as:

Being passed about too much between different people
Bright lights
Flashing toys
Loud toys
TV
Too much noise (eg. lots of loud voices)

As a baby will sleep on and off around the clock, you will find that it may be easiest to do the bedtime routine shortly before your own bedtime so that they are with you throughout the evening. Start wind-down time about 30–60 minutes before you go to bed by turning the TV off if you have it on, dimming lights, and giving them a wash down using cotton wool and warm water. After this you could offer a quick massage (ensure the room is warm) and then get them in their nightwear if they are not already in it. Ensure you offer a feed before taking them to bed, and wind them thoroughly afterwards. As you take them to their sleep space in your room, hold them in your arms or close to you so that they feel warm and safe, then place them down on their back in their cot. If they startle a little when you place them down, keep your hand on their chest. Holding their hands together, palm-to-palm, can help them relax. Keep their hands held together until you feel they are calm and then use your voice to tell them it is sleep time.

In these first couple of weeks they will wake every few hours for a feed. Keep the lights dim when feeding them in the night. Change them and wind them halfway through a feed so that if they fall asleep at the end of one, you will not need to wake them with a nappy change: you can just put them straight back down to sleep. Some babies, especially bottle-fed babies, will need some light winding at the end of the feed. You can do this by placing them over your shoulder and rubbing or lightly patting their back.

Remember: your baby does not know the difference between night and day for quite some time yet, so frequent night wakes are normal.

SLEEP NEEDS

Babies have varying nap requirements, but typically you can expect the following:

Age	Number of naps	Total duration of daytime naps
0–3 months	Regular naps/feeds throughout the day. Short periods of being awake	Regular naps/feeds throughout the day. Short periods of being awake
3–6 months	3–4	4–5 hours
6–9 months	3	3–4 hours
9–18 months	2	2–3 hours
18–36 months	Up to 1 nap	Up to 2 hours
36 months–school starters	Some babies still require a nap depending on energy expended during the day	No more than 1 hour

The nap guide table is helpful to try and understand if your baby is having too little or too much sleep during the day. However, some babies are catnappers and will have short naps during the day and manage well on this. These babies will usually make up for their sleep at night-time, so if you have a baby that is having less than these amounts and sleeping well at night, as well as being alert and happy in the day, then it really is nothing to worry about.

Be aware though that if they are only ever having short naps of 20–30 minutes, it may be a sign that early sleep cues were missed.

When it comes to dropping naps, you will often find that a baby becomes difficult to settle at a certain nap. There is no harm in giving them restful time in their cot at their usual nap time if they are quite content, but if they become disgruntled by this, see if they can manage without the nap. It may be that other naps need to be earlier or later in the day to allow them to adjust. When children begin to drop naps, it doesn't need to be something you fear. In fact, it can bring you greater freedom in your day, especially when they drop the daytime nap entirely between 18 months and 3 years old. This often really worries parents but you will no longer need to plan your day around their nap! Remember that it is OK, even after they drop a nap, if they occasionally still need one. Increased activity levels in a day may mean they require the nap every now and again and you will just adjust subsequent naps accordingly. This is particularly important for children who are only on one nap a day and drop to no naps. Many toddlers will need a small nap during the day every now and again, even if it is only 20–30 minutes to recharge!

The next table shows overall sleep requirements by age in a 24-hour period. Bear in mind that even if a baby has multiple wake ups in the night, it doesn't affect them like it does us, as adults. So if they go to bed at 8pm and then wake at 6am, this would be classed as 10 hours' sleep even if they wake 3–4 times in the night for feeds or to be resettled. If, however, they are awake for long periods at night (over an hour) this would have an effect on the total sleep.

Age	Average sleep needed in 24 hours
0–6 weeks	Regular naps/feeds over a 24-hour period
6–12 weeks	14–18 hours
3–6 months	13–16 hours
6–9 months	12–16 hours
9–18 months	11–15 hours
18–36 months	12–14 hours
36 months–5 years	10–13 hours

CLOTHING

The chart below is a guide for what to dress your baby in based on room temperature. When it is around 19–20C, be mindful of the temperature the room drops to in the early hours (when houses are typically coolest.)

WHAT SHOULD I DRESS MY BABY IN?

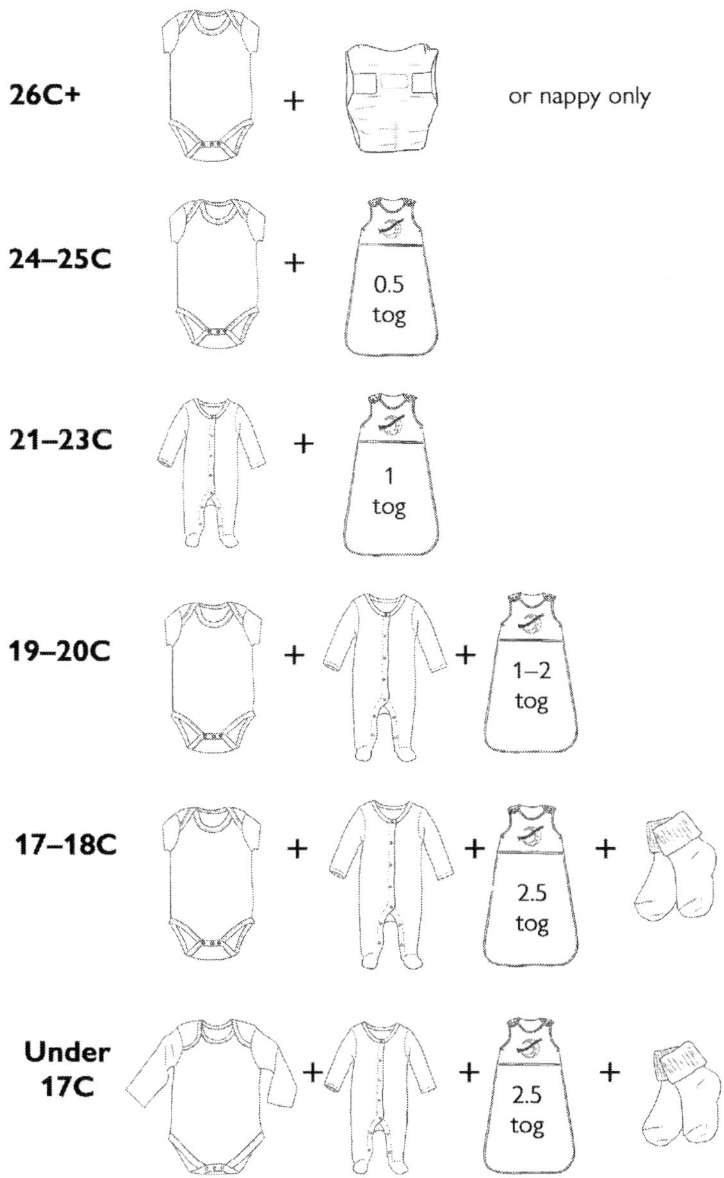

100% cotton clothing is ideal for a baby and, more recently, bamboo clothing is becoming more popular due to its sustainability, breathability and durability. Both cotton and bamboo clothing will keep them warm, but also keep them cool if the room is warm. For young babies who still have multiple nappy changes at night, nightdresses are a great item of clothing as they can be pulled up easily without needing to undo zips or poppers which can wake a baby. Nappy changes are possible to do when a baby is asleep and shouldn't wake them completely if done in a dimly lit, calm environment.

Some clothing comes with huge labels that can be itchy for your baby. If this is the case, remove them.

Dress your baby according to the room temperature. In colder temperatures (under 17C), dress your baby in multiple layers. If they become too warm, you can easily take layers off without waking them too much.

Top tip: if the temperature dips low in the room overnight, consider socks under the babygrow. In warmer temperatures, it may be appropriate just to dress your baby in a nappy or a vest.

SOCKS FOR SLEEP

For those of you who are familiar with my sleep methods, you will know that one of my number one tips (so simple but can be so effective) is to dress your baby in socks at night (unless the room is incredibly warm.) Wearing socks can help prevent early hours wake-ups (not wake-ups for hunger). Feet and hands are the first part of the body to get cold. Having said that, you should never rely on the temperature of your baby's hands or feet to tell how hot or cold they are. The back of their neck or chest is a fairly reliable gauge. Putting socks on your baby can help regulate the temperature of the feet, preventing them getting cold, which can wake them when they go into a lighter phase of sleep. So if your baby is having a wake-up around 2–5am, and it is not for milk, consider socks at night and see if it does the trick. Between 2 and 5am is typically when a house and one's body temperature are at their coolest.

NAPPIES

For babies who are drinking larger volumes of milk at their last feed (babies over about 3 months of age or drinking more than 7oz), nappies with an expandable waistband (such as pull-ups) can be beneficial as they won't feel tight on their tummy as it expands, or when it becomes loose as they empty their bladder in the night.

HATS AND HANDS

You must not cover a baby's head for sleep. As heat escapes from a baby's head, covering it may cause overheating.

Hands do not need to be covered unless there is a medical reason for it, such as a baby suffering from eczema and potentially itching themselves and cutting their face or body with their nails. Lots of babies use their hands for comfort at night by bringing them to their mouth or rubbing their face. Covering them prevents a baby from being able to comfort themselves.

WHAT TO BUY

There are so many gadgets available on the market now that claim to aid sleep. The issue with the claims is that there is very rarely going to be a gadget that can settle a baby better than you can.

Be cautious of items such as mattresses, cots, fragrances, light shows or sleep pods that claim to improve sleep. Ensure that they are safe for babies and safe for sleep. Often, using items that make these claims and seeing an improvement in sleep is purely a coincidence.

Here are my recommendations for sleep-related purchases:

A firm mattress

If money is tight, let this be the one thing that you buy new. A firm mattress is really important as it provides a firm base and provides the necessary resistance for your baby to develop and strengthen muscles. A firm mattress also keeps babies on a level surface which will not block their airways. Ensure that the mattress fits well inside the cot and that there are no gaps that the baby could get stuck in.

Mattresses should be protected by a waterproof cover.

If you do buy secondhand or use a mattress that has been passed down, ensure that when it was used previously it had a waterproof cover and that it is free from any damage such as rips or tears.

Cot

A cot doesn't need to be new, but it is a safe sleep space for a baby. Ensure it is constructed correctly and that everything is tightened. If buying secondhand, ensure it is thoroughly cleaned before use. In the UK, look out for British Standard Mark BS EN 716–1.

Baby sleep bag

Although not recommended for babies under 8lbs, a sleep bag provides a warm layer for your baby. They are available in different tog levels depending on the temperature in the room and often have zips that make night-time nappy changes easier.

A red night light

I wouldn't recommend a light that stays on all night, as a baby can become reliant on it. However, if you do need a light for night-time feeds and changes, invest in one into which you can fit a red bulb. Red bulbs can be purchased online or in hardware stores, and the light it omits does not interfere with melatonin production.

Swaddles

Swaddling can be done by using thin sheets. You do not need to purchase a specific swaddle suit, although these are becoming more popular as a baby can easily be zipped into them and they are shaped in such a way that they can't be swaddled too tightly.

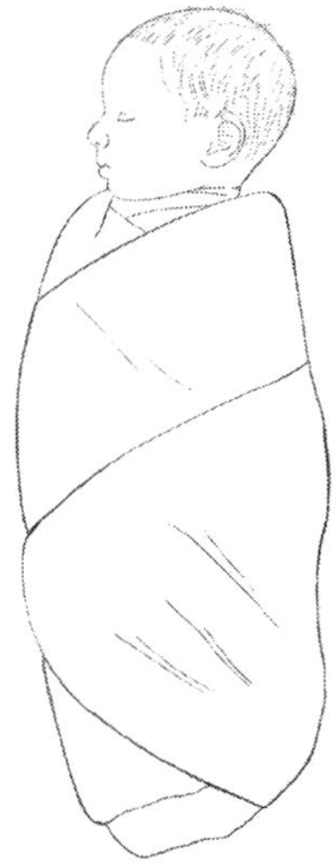

A room thermometer

Often what may feel too cool for us as adults may be the perfect temperature for a baby. The optimum temperature for a sleep environment is between 16C and 20C. Some room thermometers do omit a blue light when it is at a certain temperature, so my advice would be either to choose one that doesn't do so or make sure the light is out of sight of the baby.

A video monitor

With so many video monitors available this can be a bit of a minefield. A portable monitor is useful so that you can watch your baby from any room. Some cameras can now be paired with an app on your phone so can be viewed wherever you are.

Audio monitor

I highly recommend an audio monitor. It is very portable, and watching a video monitor constantly can increase anxiety levels. Babies move around a lot and it is often unnecessary to assist your baby when they are doing so. A lot of issues can start from going in too quickly when they are not crying and just having a wriggle around. They are usually more than capable of resettling themselves.

Cotton or bamboo babygrows

As mentioned on page 82. Soft and breathable, but cut out any itchy labels.

Nightdresses/gowns/baby bundlers

As mentioned on page 82. Useful for easy nappy changes in the night.

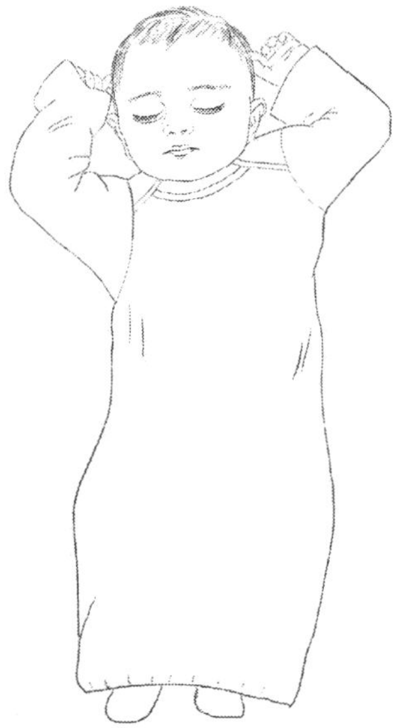

A travel cot

Although not totally necessary, a travel cot can be very useful for daytime sleeps. Moses baskets can be grown out of very quickly and a travel cot will last you years. You can also use it when staying away from home. There are many lightweight versions available and you don't need to buy new. If you are buying secondhand, ensure it is thoroughly cleaned before use and the mattress is firm and fits the cot. Ensure that all parts are tightened so there is no risk of collapse.

Baby bouncer

Lots of people buy into the idea of mechanical rocking chairs. In my experience, they can cause a baby to become very reliant on needing a rocking motion to sleep. Although there is absolutely nothing wrong with rocking your baby to sleep, it can become tiring as they grow heavier, if it has to be done for every sleep and for long durations. A baby bouncer still gives a slight rocking motion when the baby moves, but not rhythmic enough that they will learn to rely on it. The perfect place to put your baby during the day when they are awake, it is safe and allows you to be hands free in the room. A baby bouncer should not be used for sleep, however, as it is not a flat surface.

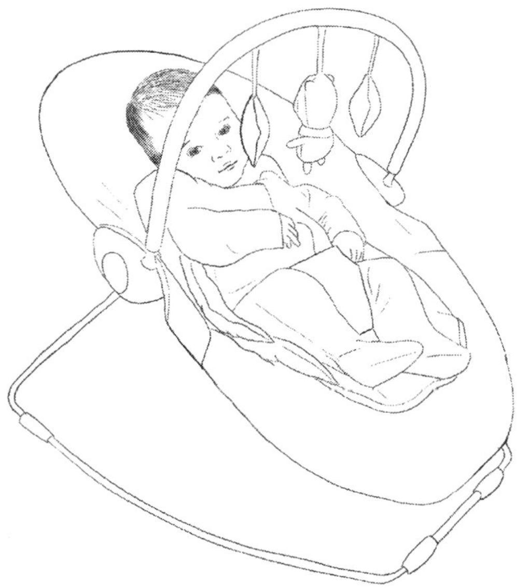

White/pink noise machine

These can be very effective for soothing a baby and helping to drown out any external noise that may disturb them.

Window covers/blackout blinds

Ensure that the windows where your baby sleeps are well covered so that the room can be made completely dark. As mentioned in much more detail on page 50, light can have a very negative effect on a baby's sleep.

Good-quality sheets

Sheets that are made from a soft, non-synthetic material will help regulate temperature and prevent any irritation or itchiness for your baby. Ensure that the sheet fits tightly on the mattress.

A comfort toy

As previously mentioned, some babies love holding and even sucking a comfort toy or blanket. This can be a useful addition when settling a child. If they are under a year old, it should not be left in the cot with them, but it can be fantastic to use when settling them for sleep or if they are upset during the daytime.

WHAT YOU DON'T NEED

Light shows

Your baby may seem mesmerised by a light show during the day when doing sensory activities but it can actually keep them awake at night if used at bedtime as it encourages them to keep their eyes focused on moving patterns.

Bright night lights

A night light may be helpful for night feeds and changes but can actually interfere with night-time sleep. Use a red night light where possible and avoid white night lights or blue lights (some products used for decongesting omit a blue light.)

Cot bumpers

Cot bumpers (even mesh versions) are not advised as babies can become caught up in them. Babies quickly learn the limits of their cot, and the consequence of getting caught up in a cot bumper is far greater than that of getting a limb caught in the bars.

Sleep pods/nests/cocoons

These are not necessary for baby sleep and are not a safe sleep space.

Mechanical rockers

As mentioned previously, they may seem helpful, but babies will quickly become reliant on this motion for sleep. They are also not a safe sleep space.

Breathing monitors

Increasingly popular in recent years, there is, however, no evidence that these devices prevent problems (such as SIDS) in healthy infants. For parents that are already anxious, a breathing monitor can increase anxiety levels unnecessarily. On the flip side, some parents may find it reassuring, so if you are considering purchasing one, think over your reasons for doing so.[36]

Pillows

While pillows are safe for adults, this is not the case for babies. They are unnecessary, as well as posing a suffocation risk. If you are to introduce a pillow for the cot, do not do so before a baby is around two years of age. Even at this age, there is no evidence to suggest that it will give a better night's sleep.

Duvets

As with pillows, these are unnecessary and pose a suffocation risk. Sleep bags are far safer as they cannot be pulled up over your baby's head. If you decide to use a duvet, try and wait until they are at least two years of age.

CO-SLEEPING & BED SHARING

It is very important when considering co-sleeping or bed sharing that you are aware of the risks and if you do choose to co-sleep, you know how you can reduce these risks as much as possible.

Co-sleeping is defined as any situation where the infant and parent are in close sensory range of each other (usually touch). It does not necessarily mean the baby is in the parental bed, as is sometimes assumed when the term is used.

BED SHARING

Bed sharing is where parents and infants sleep together in the same bed. In many cultures, sharing the parental bed is commonplace.

I would suggest doing lots of research if you are considering bed-sharing (where you share the same sleep space as your baby, so not using a side cot), as bed sharing is a significant risk factor for SIDS.

Research has shown, however, that if infant death has occurred while bed sharing, there was usually another risk factor present, such as drug use, alcohol, smoking, a pillow or duvet being used, or placing baby in the wrong position in the bed (ie. not on their back). If you do choose to bed share, it is so important that you give your baby the safest space possible.

Do not bed share if ANY of the risk factors below apply:

- If your baby was premature or of low birth weight
- If you or the person you share a bed with are a smoker (even if you do not smoke in that room)
- If you or the person you share a bed with have drunk alcohol
- If you or the person you share a bed with have taken any drugs or medication that might impair you
- If you or the person you share a bed with are extremely tired
- If you do not breastfeed your baby

The mattress must be firm. If there is any sagging due to the weight of one of the adults in the bed, you must not share with the baby as there's a risk of them rolling in the bed. Always ensure that no pillows, duvets or blankets are near the baby.

Never sleep on a sofa or armchair with your baby. It is very dangerous. With a soft surface, the baby can roll, get stuck, and even suffocate.

CO-SLEEPING (SIDE COTS)

It is becoming more and more common for parents to use a side cot attached to the parental bed as it allows the baby to have their own sleep space right next to their parents, yet still in the same sensory space of smell, touch and sight.

A side cot makes it really easy for breastfeeding mothers, as your baby is within arm's reach and you can literally slide them over to you for a feed. A side cot also makes it easy to comfort your baby in the night as you can easily reach over to them. Being so close to you will be very comforting to your baby.

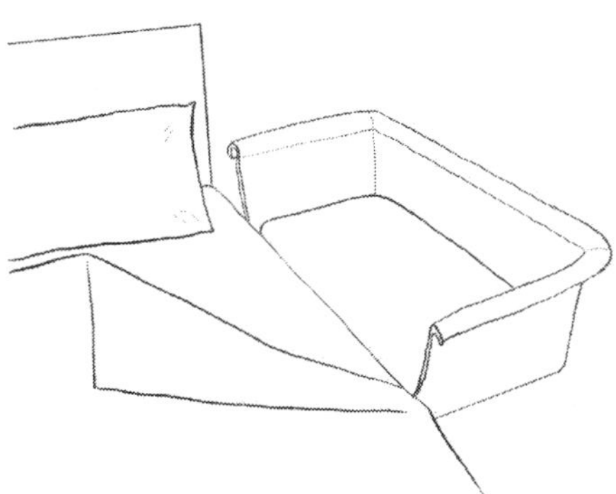

If co-sleeping with a baby, even if they are in a side cot, you must ensure that no pillows, duvets or blankets are near them. Also avoid letting pets or other small children into your bed as they may get into your baby's sleep space, which could potentially be very unsafe. Ensure that if using a side cot it is well secured, so that there is no risk of falling into a gap between your bed and theirs. You must also ensure that their side cot is not near a radiator.

If you are a smoker, have been drinking alcohol, or are on medication that may impair you, it would be safer to have your baby in a cot, as opposed to a side cot.

ADVANTAGES OF CO-SLEEPING/BED SHARING

Parents that co-sleep or bed share with their babies may have longer periods of sleep than those that don't. Although waking more often perhaps, they do not need to get out of bed to tend to their baby.

Easy access for breastfeeding babies

A baby can be placed on the breast easily to feed, or if at an age where they are more mobile, they may be able to make their own way over to the mother for a feed, sometimes not even waking the mother.

ROOM SHARING

Room sharing is by far the safest way to share the same sensory space as your baby. It enables your baby to be near you whilst being in their own sleep space. You will be able to hear them, see them and be safe in the knowledge that they in their own sleep space with no risk of blankets, covers or other children or pets interfering with their sleep and putting them at risk. When room sharing, a baby can smell your presence, as well as see you or hear you, which is very reassuring. It is recommended to room share with your baby for at least 6 months. In general, a baby will be in the parents' room when room sharing (in their cot, with the adult in their own bed) but there is nothing to say (if space allows) that the baby cannot be in their own room from day one with the adult/adults setting up camp in the baby's room. This may not be practical, but it does mean that when you decide to sleep in separate rooms, your baby is already in their familiar place. Nurseries are often set up during pregnancy with everything a baby needs, whereas an adult room generally is not.

TWINS AND MULTIPLES

Just because babies experienced the same pregnancy conditions, it does not mean their sleep patterns will be the same. Even if they are genetically identical, this is unlikely to be the case.

It is important to understand each of the baby's individual sleep needs. One may have a greater need for sleep than the other, one may be more difficult to settle. It will make it easier if you get a good routine in place, and there is no reason why you can't start doing so within a few days of coming home.

I'm not meaning that you have to be totally strict with exact times, but it will be beneficial if you try and get the babies on the same sleep and feeding schedule.

If breastfeeding and one baby feeds, then offer the other baby a feed at the same time or directly after. Tandem feeding is possible with twins, and even triplets with the right support. I would highly recommend getting support from an IBCLC who can show you how to get feeding established with two or more babies. Although breastfeeding is typically meant to be on demand, you may find that if you do this, you will be feeding constantly and there will be no time to do anything in-between. A lot of mothers who breastfeed twins and multiples will wake both babies if one wakes for a feed. You will still be feeding on demand, and never restricting feeds, but by offering the other baby a feed when one wants feeding, they will likely fall into a bit of a pattern.

If formula feeding, feed on the same schedule – a minimum of every 3 or 4 hours, and in the first few weeks possibly more often. There are some great tandem-feeding pillows available that help you feed two babies at once if you do not have assistance.

When it comes to sleep, try and get both babies down at the same time or within 10 and 15 minutes of each other. When one baby wakes from the nap, wake the other within 10 and 15 minutes. A baby chair, in which you can place one of the babies safely while you are settling the other, is a very useful item. A sling is also a great option for multiple babies, as your hands are free to hold and settle whichever baby is not in the sling. Tandem slings can be very useful too. See if there is a "sling library" local to you where you can get advice from consultants who can give you advice on the best baby carrier for your needs.

Twins often sleep better when they are closer together. Ensure that if they are in the same cot you put them either both at one end with their feet at the foot of the cot or at opposite ends with their feet touching the end. They do not need to be separated unless they disturb each other or start rolling onto one another. Once they can roll it is advisable to have them at opposite ends to give them space. They will still be able to smell each other and hear each other's breathing and reassuring noises.

If one child is tending to get disturbed by the other, try using white or pink noise to drown out noises. If this does not help, move them into separate cots.

A small percentage of twins and multiples do not sleep well together and may need a separate room as they become older. However, this is generally not the case with young babies who become used to each other's noises fairly quickly.

Consider a routine for twins and multiples. This will give you a structure to your day and theirs. You will probably find that having them on the same schedule gives you more time to yourself between feeds.

I have laid out some sample routines which you may find useful. The feeding times are for a formula-fed baby and are only a guide. You may wish to demand feed – doing so when a baby shows hunger signs – even if using formula. Breast feeding is on demand so slot it in accordingly. You could always offer the first feed of the day at the same time every day for a breastfed baby to help them try and establish a routine.

You will see that the feeds are 3–4 hourly. Babies who are of low birth weight may require feeds more often. Although you do not need to start the wake at 6/7am for first feed, if you are a parent that wants to get into a semi-routine, then doing this feed at the same time every day starts to give a bit of structure to the day. You can go back to sleep straight afterward, so don't feel it has to be the start to your day – simply a time that is likely to become so in the following months due to daylight and natural circadian rhythm.

FIRST MONTH HOME

Time		Duration (approximate)
Between 6am and 7am	Wake and feed using feed pillow. Have milk prepared before waking babies. Change baby's nappy half way through feed.	Bear in mind that if they had a large feed for the previous feed in the night, they may only want a small volume at this one. This is OK.
After feed	Winding. When you are winding one baby, place the other baby down in the feeding pillow or baby chair.	Up to 5–10 minutes per baby in early weeks or until wind is brought up.
After winding	Nap	30–90 minutes
Between 9am and 10am	Feed	
	Winding	Up to 5–10 minutes per baby in early weeks or until wind is brought up.
	Interaction	20–60 minutes
	Nap	30–90 minutes
Between 1pm and 2pm	Feed	
	Winding	Up to 5–10 minutes per baby in early weeks or until wind is brought up.
	Interaction	20–60 minutes
	Nap	30–90 minutes
Between 4pm and 5pm	Feed	
	Winding	Up to 5–10 minutes per baby in early weeks or until wind is brought up.

Time		Duration (approximate)
5.30pm	Wash/bath	5–10 minutes
	Massage	5–10 minutes
	Nap	30–90 minutes
Between 7pm & 8pm	Feed	
	Winding	Up to 5–10 minutes per baby in early weeks or until wind is brought up.
8.30pm	Calm music/singing/stories. Ensure all lights are dim and environment is calm.	
	Restful time. Baby will probably sleep on and off.	
Around 10pm or when parents go to bed	Feed	
	Winding	Up to 5–10 minutes per baby in early weeks or until wind is brought up.
After feeding/winding	Bedtime	
1am–2am	Feed (change nappy half way through feed and wind)	
	Light winding after feed by rubbing back	Until wind comes up.
	Back to sleep	
4am–6am	Feed (change nappy half way through feed and wind)	
	Light winding after feed by rubbing back	Until wind comes up.
	Back to sleep	

2–3 MONTHS

Time		Duration (approximate)
6.30am	Wake to feed	
	Wind	Until wind comes up
	Nap	30–90 minutes
10/10.30am	Feed	
	Winding	Until wind comes up
	Interaction	Until they show sleep cues
When baby shows early sleep cues	Nap	30–90 minutes
2/2.30pm	Feed	
	Winding	Until wind comes up
	Interaction	Until they show sleep cues
When baby shows early sleep cues	Nap	30–90 minutes
5.30/6pm	Feed	
	Winding	Until wind comes up
6.30pm	Wash/bath	5–10 minutes
	Massage	5–10 minutes
7pm	Interaction/catnap	Around 30 minutes
7.30pm	Wind-down time. Dimmed lights, minimal light interference from TVs etc.	
8pm	Feed	
	Wind	Until wind comes up
8.30pm	Bedtime	
10/11pm	Feed (change nappy half way through)	
	Wind and back to bed	
2/3am	Feed (change nappy half way through)	
	Wind and back to bed	

4–5 MONTHS

Time		Duration (approximate)
Between 6am and 7am	Feed	
After feed	Winding. When you are winding one baby, place the other baby in the feeding pillow or baby bouncer	5 minutes
After winding	Up for the day and some light interaction	30–90 minutes
Between 8 and 9am or when they show early sleep cues	Nap	30–90 minutes
Between 10am and 11am	Feed	
	Wind	5 minutes
	Interaction	30–90 minutes
Between 12 and 1pm or when they show early sleep cues	Nap	60–120 minutes
Between 2pm and 3pm	Feed	
	Winding	5 minutes
	Interaction	30–90 minutes
Between 4pm and 5pm	Nap	Up to 1 hour
Between 6pm and 7pm	Wash/bath	10–15 minutes
	Massage	5–15 minutes
After bath and massage	Feed	
	Wind	Until wind comes up

Time		Duration (approximate)
Between 6.30pm and 7.30pm or when they show early sleep cues	Bedtime	
Between 10pm and 11pm	Feed	If required
Early hours	Feed	If required

Bath time can be a juggling act with multiple babies. It is important to always be present in the room when they are in the bath. Do not leave them, even for a moment. In the first few months, if you have someone who can help at bathtime it can be really helpful. When babies come out of the bath they tend to cry due to the sudden temperature change. Have towels warmed and ready, and dry them off quickly so they don't get cold. Whichever room you dress them in, ensure that it is nice and warm and that there are no drafts.

If you feel more comfortable bathing them one at a time then do so. Bathing them together once they have more head control and can sit up can be more fun and less stressful than trying to do two or more at once. Have everything ready if you are on your own such as towels, nappies, wipes, any creams needed, clothing and a chair in which you can put one of the babies. That way, you'll have everything you need to be in the room the whole time.

6–9 MONTHS (establishing food)

Don't introduce all meals at once and try and introduce the late meal of the day last to ensure it doesn't cause digestive discomfort and interfere with night-time sleep. The meal timings are a guide.

Time		Duration (approximate)
Between 6am and 7am	Milk feed	
After feed	Winding	Until wind comes up
8am	Breakfast	
Between 8am and 9am	Nap	Up to 1.5 hours
When they wake	Milk feed	
	Winding	Until wind comes up
	Interaction	
Between 12pm and 1pm	Lunch	
When sleep cues are shown	Nap	Up to 2 hours
When they wake	Milk feed	
	Winding	Until wind comes up
	Interaction	
Around 4pm	Dinner	

Time		Duration (approximate)
After dinner	Nap	Some babies will still require 3 naps a day so if they need to nap at this time then let them have a short nap of around 30 minutes. Bear in mind that if they do so, they may require a later bedtime, closer to 7.30pm.
5.30pm	Wash/bath	10–15 minutes
	Massage	5–15 minutes
6pm	Milk feed	
	Winding	Until wind comes up
Between 6.30pm and 7.30pm or when they show early sleep cues	Bedtime	
During the night	Milk feed	If required

As food becomes more established you may find that your baby goes off milk a bit, particularly if formula-fed. Solid food will be keeping them fuller for longer, but do remember that milk is still their main source of nutrition until 12 months old, so ensure that they aren't getting too full up on food and then rejecting all milk feeds.

10 MONTHS–24 MONTHS

During this time, nap needs can vary considerably so focus on your baby's sleep cues to understand how much sleep they need during the day. In general, most babies will still require two naps until around 18 months of age. But, saying that, some 12-month-old babies will function well on just one nap (perhaps requiring an earlier bedtime so they don't become overtired). With twins you may find, one of them may need two naps, and the other just one.

By 10 months, when a baby may be beginning to crawl and certainly be more upright most of the time, you shouldn't need to wind them as much. They should be fairly efficient at bringing wind up themselves. But don't assume that they will never need winding again. If they seem uncomfortable, try giving them a little rub on the back and see if that helps, if they are unsettled after a feed.

Time		Duration (approximate)
Between 6am and 8am	Milk feed	
8am	Breakfast	
	Interaction	
	Snacks	
Around 10am	Nap	Up to 1 hour
Around 12/1pm	Lunch	
After lunch	Milk (for younger babies) then Nap	Up to 2 hours or 2.5 if only one nap
When they wake	Interaction	
Around 4pm (gradually take this later as they become older and drink less milk)	Dinner	
	Interaction	
5.30pm	Wash/bath	10–15 minutes
	Massage	5–15 minutes
6pm	Milk feed	
	Interaction	
Between 6.30pm and 7.30pm or when they show early sleep cues	Bedtime	
During the night	Milk feed	If required

Milk feeding at night-time may still be appropriate for some babies. The World Health Organization states that breastfed babies may still require feeds up until around two years of age, or even older if they demand it.

Once your baby is 12 months old, solid food becomes the main source of nutrients, but a baby will still require plenty of calcium in their diet, so milk is still advised. You may find that a baby is quite happy to just have a feed of milk in the morning and before bed. A breastfed baby may have a few other feeds during the day, as breastfeeding is about thirst and comfort as well as hunger. That being said, when a baby is not feeling well you may find that they want some more milk feeds (even from a bottle) as it is comforting for them.

SPECIAL CARE BABIES

Sometimes babies need a little help after birth in intensive care or special care, and this itself can mean your baby has different sleep needs.

Special care and NICU are generally very "busy" environments, and I don't mean busy as in a lot of people (even though there can be quite a few), but rather as in a lot of stimulus. Beeping from machines, various coloured lights around the room, babies' cries and general chitter chatter between nurses and parents is constant. Because of this, babies who have spent time in special care and are used to noise around them have become desensitised to it. When they go home, a very quiet environment may feel strange to them. As a result, they often like hearing noise going on around them from those in the house.

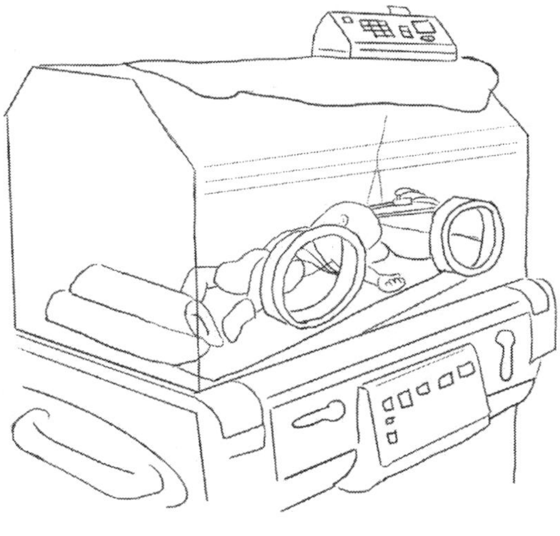

In these hospital environments, nurses will actively encourage parents to be involved with their baby's day-to-day care as much as possible, encouraging skin to skin time or "kangaroo care" for babies and the option to feed your baby if possible. Breastfeeding is encouraged to be on demand, and formula feeding will usually be on a more schedule-based regime, which is usually every 3–4 hours upon discharge.

If your baby is premature, even if you have decided that you want to formula feed your baby, consider colostrum harvesting. Colostrum is the first form of milk produced during pregnancy and for the first few days after birth. There seems to be a huge misconception that women produce mature breast milk immediately, and this can often lead to the mother feeling that she isn't capable of producing milk, when it actually takes a few days for your milk to come in. In the period between birth and when your breast milk comes in, which is usually around days 2–4, colostrum is produced. It is a yellowish, thick and sticky liquid which is produced in very small volumes.

Colostrum harvesting is where you hand-express the colostrum from the breast into a syringe, or onto a sterile spoon. You may only produce a few drops of this the first time you try it, but if you can try a few times a day, you should see the volume increase to a few millilitres. Bear in mind that a teaspoon of colostrum is enough for a feed for a newborn baby. It can be stored in the fridge or freezer if you choose to do this before birth, and it has so many benefits, especially for sick or premature babies, as it contains antibodies that help fight infections, loads of nutrients, and is high in protein. It is also hugely beneficial for babies with jaundice, as it works as a laxative which will help rid the body of bilirubin.

If you plan on breastfeeding, be assured that colostrum should be all your baby needs. They shouldn't need to be topped up with formula unless there is a medical need for it. Your milk will come in quicker the more you stimulate your breasts to harvest the colostrum or the more you get your baby to feed. Ask for breastfeeding support if you feel concerned at any point. Colostrum also helps regulate blood sugars. If formula top ups are being suggested for your baby and you wish to solely give your baby breast milk, ask staff about whether donor breast milk may be an option instead of formula until your milk supply increases.

Many premature babies will be placed to sleep on their front when in special care/NICU. Although this goes against safe sleep guidelines, what we have to remember is that these babies are monitored 24/7, unlike at home, so it is safe for them to be on their tummies in hospital. Lying in this position is the closest to how they were in the womb, and it also helps facilitate growth in the newborn, promotes proper skeletal alignment, and decreases skin injuries. Babies sleeping on their tummy also tend to sleep deeper, which may be beneficial for them in hospital, if they are unwell as most recovery is done while asleep. This should NEVER be a reason to sleep them on their tummy at home, as sleeping too deeply can actually pose a risk if they have underlying conditions and has been shown to increase the risk of SIDS.[37]

Once your baby has graduated from all the tubes and wires, and is gaining weight sufficiently, they will be transitioned to the safe sleep position on their back so that they are used to it when they go home. If you are ever concerned that this is not the case, speak to the nurse in charge about transitioning to back-sleeping before discharge.

Chapter 7

AIDING SLEEP

SLEEP ASSOCIATIONS

A sleep association is a sequence of events or an act that a baby will associate with sleep. I generally break down sleep associations into three categories: positive, neutral and negative associations. Your opinion may differ on how I have categorised them, but to give you an idea, this is how I describe the categories:

Positive sleep associations
An act or a sequence of events that can be carried out with ease by the main caregiver or someone else, and is maintainable long-term.

Neutral sleep associations
May be deemed by some as an act that is maintainable, but by others (who perhaps have other children or the demands of work etc.) not to be so in the long-term.

Negative sleep associations
An act or sequence of events that is not maintainable long-term and may require the same caregiver every time to carry out the act. Without this act or caregiver, the baby will not sleep without protest.

POSITIVE SLEEP ASSOCIATIONS

Feeding to sleep
Feeding to sleep is natural. It is nature's way of being able to comfort and settle a baby, and many parents use this as a very successful method to settle their baby to sleep. It doesn't need to be breastfeeding your baby to sleep either. You may choose to combination feed your baby, feed

expressed breast milk in a bottle, or formula feed. Whichever method you use, it will bring comfort to your baby.

Reading a book to your child

Babies love to listen, and a familiar story every night can become very enjoyable for them. It doesn't need to be the same story every night; choose from a range of three or four so that the stories become familiar. They quickly start to associate pictures or words from the final pages with the fact that bedtime comes after these words/pictures.

Singing

Singing can be very soothing for your baby and you may even find that they try to join in. Have lots of eye contact with them when doing so. They will watch your mouth movements and you will probably get a few smiles. Watch out for them beginning to lose interest as this is an early sleep cue – a sign that you can put them down to sleep. Carry on your singing, though, as you place them down, giving a smooth transition.

White noise, pink noise or lullabies

All of these can be played for your baby while you are not present, which makes them an excellent sleep association. Anyone can put them on, and they won't have to stay with the baby as it settles itself to sleep.

Swaddling

As mentioned on page 124, swaddling can be a very effective method for settling a baby to sleep due to restricting the startle reflex in young babies.

Dark environment

A dark environment helps trigger the production of the sleep hormone melatonin. Dark rooms can be recreated at other people's homes if you are away, and even in prams with pram covers if your baby is having a nap out of the house. (Pram covers must be breathable, and I wouldn't advise covering a pram during warm weather.)

Massage

Not all babies love massage but a large number of them do! Massage doesn't need to be complicated. See pages 112–114 for a few massage techniques.

NEUTRAL SLEEP ASSOCIATIONS

Baby wearing (slings)

Babies love feeling close to you. It makes them feel warm and safe and the beat of your heart will be comforting. Baby wearing has shown to be particularly beneficial for babies suffering with reflux or colic-like symptoms.

The only issue which may arise is the baby becoming reliant on being very close to you for all sleeps, so try to ensure not all daytime sleeps are in the sling/wrap.

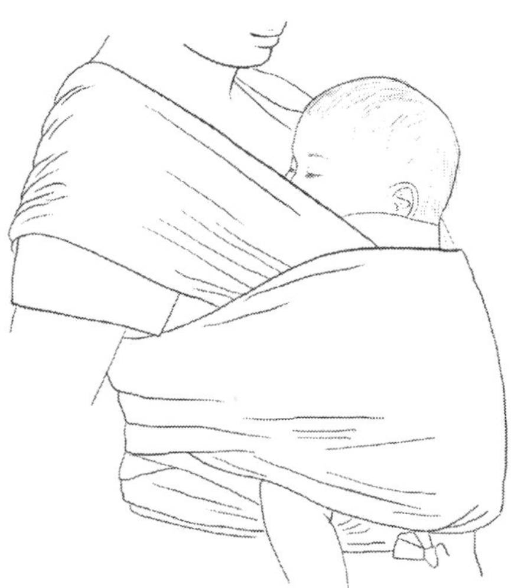

Bath

Baths are very much a love it or hate it scenario. Many babies will love a bath before bedtime, yet for some it will be the beginning of huge meltdowns in the evening. Babies under the age of two cannot regulate their own body temperature, so try and avoid baths within two hours of bedtime if you have a baby who wakes between bedtime and midnight many times or if you have a baby who doesn't enjoy baths. The last thing you want to do is have them stressed out before bedtime. If your baby becomes quite stressed in the bath, you could try co-bathing with your baby. This will give them lots more confidence as you are in there with them and they can be close to you.

Remember that a bath is not a necessity every night; a baby's skin is actually very sensitive so the water can sometimes have a negative effect and dry the skin out. Ensure that if you do not bath your baby, you give them a little wash down all over so they are clean. This can be done with cotton wool and warm water and a little soap if required.

Dummy/pacifier

A dummy (sometimes referred to as a pacifier) can be a great sleep association as it can be incredibly soothing for a baby. Lots of babies suck to relax themselves. Dummies may however become a negative sleep association if it is causing multiple wakes when it falls out, with you needing to replace it constantly, or in toddler-age children when they throw it out of their cot to get your attention.

Sucking

Some babies are "sucky babies" and feel very comforted when sucking anything. This can often be a dummy, but as they become a bit older, some children will suck on their fingers or a muslin or blanket and find great comfort from it. I am sure you have seen children who carry around a blanket with them and suck their thumb whilst having a blanket in their hand for comfort. These children were likely "sucky babies". Always useful to have a few duplicates of the blanket to allow you to be able to wash and rotate them frequently, as this type of baby can become very attached to their blanket or muslin and be reluctant to be without it at any point!

Rocking in arms

As mentioned earlier, rocking is a very successful way of settling a baby but as they get heavier it is less maintainable. For twins and multiples this can be very difficult to do if you are on your own, and can become unsafe if you try to hold two babies at once when you are very tired and they are getting heavier!

Only settling in arms

There is nothing wrong with settling your baby to sleep in your arms, it is a very natural thing to do, but try and get your baby down in their cot before they have fallen into a deep sleep in your arms, otherwise if they wake in the night, they may require you to pick them up and hold them to get back to sleep.

Walking in a pram

Taking your baby for some fresh air is really good for them and it is no issue for your baby to have an occasional nap in a pram. However, if your baby will only nap in the pram, this is not maintainable. Especially when it is raining outside or they need resettling at 2am and you have to take them for a walk around the neighbourhood.

NEGATIVE SLEEP ASSOCIATIONS

Driving in a car

Similar to being in a pram, this is not maintainable, especially in the middle of the night.

Sleep nests/cocoons

Not only are sleep nests/cocoons unsafe for sleep, but what I commonly see happen is a baby gets used to it for daytime sleeps and then they are not able to sleep without it at night-time, which is unsafe. Guidelines state that a baby must be accompanied when in a sleep nest or cocoon. This means that you need to be awake at all times and nearby when they are in one.

Mechanical rocking chairs/gadgets

While these can be soothing for a baby, it is not practical for this to be the only way that your baby learns to fall asleep. In the daytime this shouldn't pose too much issue and may give you that extra pair of hands that you need, but in the middle of the night, if this is the only way they can be resettled, it is not maintainable.

BEDTIME ROUTINE

This can be started from birth with your baby, and it doesn't necessarily need to be long and drawn out either. A bedtime routine is a sequence of events that you do every single evening before bed. When done consistently, your baby will learn that this sequence of events comes before their night-time sleep. A routine should be calming for a baby so any loud sounds and flashing lights should not be included. A few things that you can add into a bedtime routine are:

A bath

Bear in mind not to have it too close to bedtime due to temperature regulation (see page 110).

Bedtime story/stories

Although young babies can't speak, they are like little sponges and take in every word we are saying to them.

Singing songs/listening to music

Babies love the sound of their parent's voices, especially singing. As they become older they will likely join in with you. Relaxing music can help a baby calm down in the evening.

A massage

You don't need to take part in any baby massage courses for this. Use light and medium pressure on your baby (with lotion or olive oil) to rub, stroke or apply moveable pressure on your baby's body.

RELAXING BEDTIME MASSAGE

Carry out the massage in a warm room.

Remove your baby's clothes and ideally the nappy too although this isn't absolutely necessary. Ensure you protect the area underneath the baby if you do take the nappy off by laying down a soft towel.

Have ambient lighting in the room.

Warm some baby massage oil or olive oil in your hands, ensuring it is all over your hands and fingertips.

Start with your baby's feet. Massage the heels up to the toes. Use the palm of your hand to stroke the soles and tops of their feet. Do not pull at the toes but massage each one gently one by one.

Work up the leg, from the foot up to the thigh, and massage with light pressure over the calves and thighs as you go.

After you have done the legs, work on their arms. Starting with their hands (do similar to what you did to their feet), use gentle circular motions, working up their arms.

On their chest, use gentle stroking motions.

Next the tummy. Remember this is a delicate area so avoid even slight pressure. Let your hands gently glide over their tummy.

When massaging the face and neck (not all babies like this), use gentle stroking motions. Run your finger from the forehead and down the centre of the nose. You may find that this encourages the baby to close their eyes.

Now to the back. Younger babies may not like this as it can mean time on their tummy, but you could hold them in your arms to take the pressure away from their tummy. Use gentle strokes or gentle pressure on their back and work downwards. If they are not keen on having their back massaged, you don't have to do it, or you could do it first so that they end the massage in a more relaxed state.

I LOVE YOU MASSAGE (FOR COLIC, GASSY TUMMIES AND CONSTIPATION)

Carry out the massage in a warm room.

Remove your baby's clothes, and ideally the nappy too, although this isn't absolutely necessary. Ensure you protect the area underneath the baby if you do take the nappy off by laying down a towel.

Have ambient lighting in the room then place your baby down on their back. Warm some baby massage oil or olive oil in your hands, ensuring it is all over your hands and fingertips.

"I" Using your index finger and middle finger, place them gently on the top right side (as you view it) of your baby's abdomen. Gently trace your fingers vertically down, applying light pressure. Remember, the tummy area is very sensitive so don't press too hard.

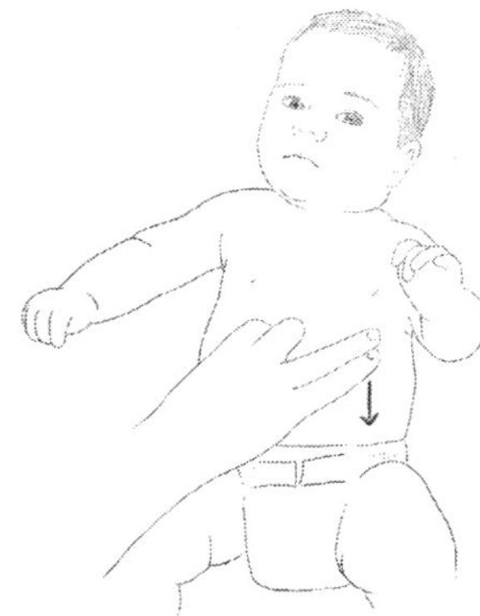

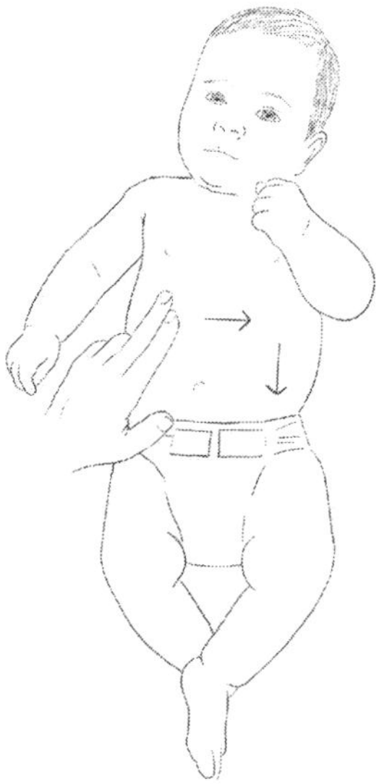

"L" Using the same two fingers, starting at the top left of the baby's abdomen (as you view it), trace your fingers from left to right and then down. Be very gentle, as you were with the "I" motion.

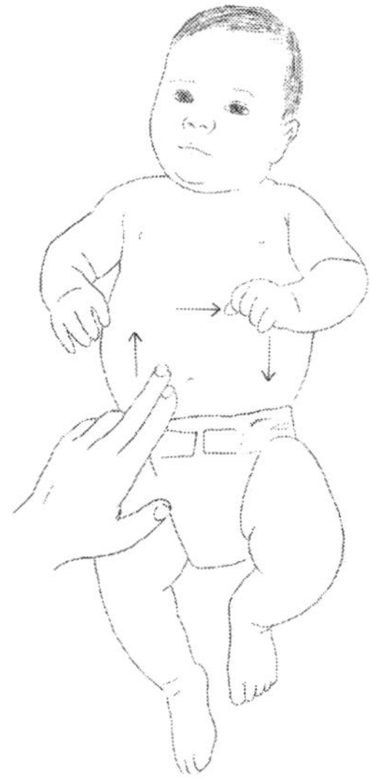

"U" Again using two fingers, starting at the bottom left of your baby's abdomen (as you view it), trace your fingers up, using gentle pressure to the top left of their abdomen then over to the top right and then down to the bottom right (an upside down U).

Repeat these steps a few times. Move your fingers slowly as this should be relaxing for your baby but will also help to move any trapped gas through the intestines.

DUMMY OR NO DUMMY?

Dummies (pacifiers) are quite controversial. Some people love the idea of them and for others they may feel that it is a definite no-no.

Some research does show that use of a dummy can reduce the risk of SIDS.[39] Babies use their suck reflex to comfort themselves, so a dummy can be very soothing for a baby. They can help you to have an aid which can be used to calm your baby, meaning your baby does not constantly need to be held.

If you are breastfeeding, try not to introduce a dummy before 6 weeks or until breastfeeding and your milk supply is well established. This is because it can cause confusion and reduce the amount a baby feeds from you. When your baby feeds from you, it actually helps to increase your milk supply.

Whether or not you use a dummy is a personal decision. As previously mentioned, although they can be soothing for a child, do bear in mind that dummies can be the cause of night wakes as babies and toddlers rarely have the ability to put their own dummy back in at night.

If you do have a baby whose dummy is falling out in the night and if you are unwilling to ditch the dummy, try a different teat size or brand as some may suit them better than others.

Below is a gentle removal technique for a dummy, making it less appealing to them. You can do this over the period of a week or so, during the day, using a new dummy each day (once the dummy has holes in it, bacteria can grow and you will be unable to clean inside the teat).

Days 1 and 2: use a pin to prick a few tiny holes in the dummy.

Days 3 and 4: using scissors, cut a couple of small slits in the dummy. Your baby will probably give a very confused look when they suck on it, but will likely still use it.

Days 5 and 6: cut bigger slits in the dummy. At this point they will probably start to go off it.

Days 7 and 8: cut off the top of the teat (just a few millimetres down from the top). It is very likely at this point that they will discard it.

Phasing it out with this holes technique will not work with all children, so if this method doesn't help, the only other way I have found to be successful quickly when getting rid of a dummy is to go cold turkey. It should only take 24–48 hours to break the habit.

For children over two, you may be able to reason with them if they can understand (some will understand better than others) and you could tell them the dummy fairy is taking them away (in exchange for a token gift) or that you need to give the dummies away to the new babies and explain to them that they are no longer a baby and don't need it anymore. Around certain celebrations of the year, for example at Christmas, you could say that they leave their dummies on the Christmas tree during the day (like decorations) and then on Christmas Eve Santa will take the dummies away and exchange them for a gift.

A very successful method I found with my twins was using a mug tree (designed to put mugs on in the kitchen) and telling them that the dummy must go on the "dummy tree" during the day. This greatly reduced the reliance on them and they found it really fun to do.

Don't remove a dummy when your child is unwell or going through any significant changes such as starting nursery or parents going back to work. Wait until they are settled or well again.

WHEN BABIES CRY

Babies cry. This is a fact. No matter which gentle method you choose when working on a baby's sleep, there will be tears at some point. I always encourage you to support your baby when they are crying, by being present in the room and calming them.

Crying is their way of alerting you that they need tending to, which could be for numerous reasons. Although I would never judge someone who chooses to use controlled crying methods, as there may be various reasons why they choose to go down this route, I believe that there are many other sleep methods that can be used with a baby that do not require them to be left to cry for periods of time alone.

Remember, too, that crying is your baby communicating with you, and they are not necessarily in distress. There is a very clear difference between leaving your baby to cry using a cry it out method (only stopping crying once exhausted) and allowing your baby to cry a little and grumble to themselves for a few moments as they settle themselves.

A lot of babies make quite a bit of noise when trying to settle themselves. Almost like a protest, they can shout, cry out and grumble.

There is a very clear difference between settling themselves and feeling stressed. With the latter, they may be going red-faced or their crying is very loud and rhythmic. Some children, if crying hysterically, will start coughing, which is often a sign of them trying to catch their breath. Or they produce a lot of dribble or mucus from their nose or mouth and may even get so hysterical that they are sick. Clearly if a child is showing any of these behaviours, they must be tended to. Although there is no current evidence to suggest that it has any long-term damage to a child, this kind of crying is clearly showing that they are unable to settle themselves and there will be a reason. Very often this may be for comfort, but do the check:

Are they fed?
Are they too cold?
Are they too hot?
Are they irritated by any clothing?
Have they been winded?
Are they unwell?
Is their happy tank full?

If any of these needs need tending to then do it. A baby who has any of these issues will not settle well at all and may have many subsequent wakes, even if they fall asleep due to being tired.

Of course if they are unwell, this is not necessarily something that you can instantly fix, so they may require extra comfort or even medication in some situations.

I talk often about the "happy tank". We always ensure that their tummy is full, but what about their happy tank? Ensure, before bedtime especially, that their emotional needs have been met. Encourage lots of smiles and engagement. Interact with them and show affection to your child to fill up their happy tank.

Any other reason for crying, such as needing comfort, being overtired, being under tired etc., can be worked on by carrying out various exercises, which I will cover separately.

It is very important in my experience never to let a child get so worked up that they vomit as this can become habitual for them. Their gag reflex is very weak when young, and I find that once a child has done it a few times it can be quite a difficult habit to undo. If your child does start this, ensure that minimal fuss is made when it happens. Remove the baby from the sleep area and clean them down, ensuring if they have been sick on themselves that they are given clean clothes. If it is in their hair, clean this up too. Clean the bed, so ensure that you have a couple of sets of clean bedding available and also a waterproof mattress protector. Avoid getting upset yourself and be as calm as you can. Reassure your little one and keep the environment as dimly lit as possible for them, and get them back in bed as soon as possible.

Chapter 8

SETTLING TECHNIQUES

You may wonder why this is not earlier on in the book when the most common question I get is, "how do I settle my baby?".

Well, the answer is that nobody knows better than you how to settle your baby. We all have our ways to get our baby to calm down. It may be a few light pats on the back, it may be pacing the house with them in your arms for 10 minutes, it may be that you feed them to settle them. There is no wrong or right answer.

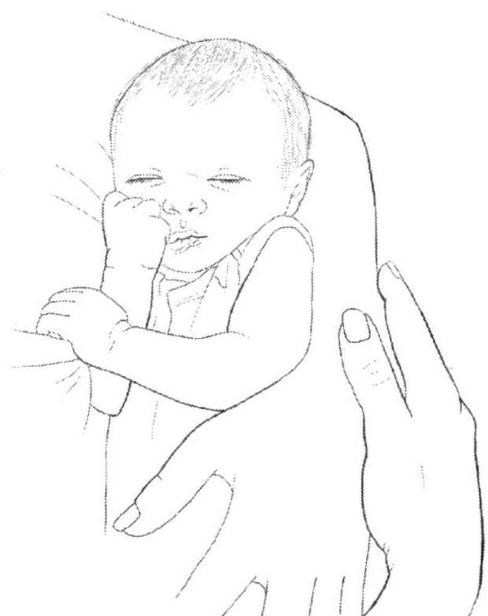

There are a few techniques you can try that may be helpful to settle your little one. There is no secret to them. You only need to do a quick search on the internet and these methods will come up. The main point I want to get across with this book, though, is that there is so much more to baby sleep than just being able to put them down to sleep. We have to ensure that all their other needs are met before a baby will be happy to go down on their own. To remind you, this is the checklist you need to go over before even beginning to try and put your baby down to sleep:

Are they fed?
Are they too cold?
Are they too hot?
Are they irritated by any clothing?
Have they been winded?
Are they unwell?
Is their happy tank full?

Ensure you are also watching for their sleep cues to get them down at the right time.

If you feel that you are not in the position at this point to be able to leave your baby without there being lots of crying, here are a few methods you can try.

Note that some of these techniques may involve your baby crying, but they will never be left alone to cry, ever. Gentle methods always involve supporting your child by being nearby so that they know that you are there to help them.

I would always encourage to carry out the "cot comfort exercise", on page 161, for a week before doing any of these techniques. That way, your child becomes more comfortable with being in their cot and doesn't associate it just with feeling upset.

PICK UP, PUT DOWN

This technique involves being continuously with your baby in the same room for as long as is needed until they realise that they are safe and secure and naturally fall asleep.

Place your baby down in their cot when drowsy. If they grumble or protest a bit, allow them to. As mentioned before, there is a huge difference between protesting or just having a moan and crying their eyes out because they are stressed. Most babies will make some noise before they go to sleep. They may shout, they may make noises like they are crying, but the difference is that it will not escalate.

If they get distressed at any point or start to cry with tears, pick them up, reassure them by cuddling them or holding them tightly, and reassure them with your voice. Once calm, place them back down in their cot. This may need to be repeated quite a few times but it is a very gentle technique to use.

PUT DOWN, NO PICK UP

Very much like the pick up, put down technique, but this time you do not pick them up. If they become upset, reassure them using your voice and your hand on them. If they are of an age where they are unable to sit or stand up in their cot, you can lean over to them. If, however, they are of an age where they can stand or reach up towards you, ensure you do not stand over them as this will only encourage them to reach up to you and stress them out. If you have a cot with bars, sit next to it and reach your arm through them, if needed. If your baby is reasonably calm and doesn't require your touch, just be near the cot, at a level equal or lower to them.

The shush, pat technique can be useful in this situation, where you use your voice to shush your baby and pat them gently in a steady rhythm at the same time. As they start to settle to sleep, slow down the patting and decrease the amount you use your voice to shush them, until they are asleep.

I'M RIGHT HERE

A lot of children get upset when they know you are leaving them. Ensure that you are playing games of peek-a-boo during the day to help your child understand that just because they can't see you, it doesn't mean you are not nearby.

Start by using the "put down, no pick up" technique but aim to be able to leave the room before they fall asleep so that if they wake in the night it is not a shock that you are not there. Start next to their cot, and tell them you are there. Once you feel they are settling, move away a few steps but ensure that you are still at a level equal or lower to them so a chair to sit on may be useful at this point. If at any point they show that they are upset by your moving away, tell them "I'm right here" and move back to where you were at the previous step. It may be that, for a few nights, you can only move a couple of steps away, but once you feel that they are content with your reassuring them from a slight distance, move further away. Continue this until you are able to leave the room while they are awake, yet drowsy. It is so important not to try and step away too quickly, or go from being near the cot to straight out the door. A steady approach will work much better long-term.

THE FLOOR BED

This may sound crazy to some, but in so many countries the floor bed is actual common practice. Lots of babies all over the world sleep near their parents for a very long time. In Japan, a baby will generally sleep next to their parent until the next child is born and, even then, they will often sleep with an adult until around ten years of age.

In the UK, the majority of babies are moved to their own room at six months and it is seen to be the norm for them to be away from their parent. Many cultures would look at this as being very strange, as they have their babies next to them for a very long time and to them this is the norm.

The floor bed may be an option if your baby struggles to be away from you yet you are reluctant to have them next to your bed anymore. Placing a mattress on the floor in their room allows the baby to be near their parent – and for the parent also, to have a restful and reasonably comfortable night's sleep. This could be an option to try if you find that it is difficult to move your child away from you and if they are unhappy to be away from you. It can be used as a temporary measure or something more permanent if needed. So often, parents move a baby into the parental bed in the middle of the night when tired, whereas this solution enables the baby to stay in their sleep space and, once you are both ready, the parent can move back to their room. This way it instills in the baby the understanding that their room is where they should be.

Wakeful periods for babies are often phases that pass, so this can be a successful solution without too much interception required. If your baby stirs (and it is not for a feed), stay laying down and try and resettle them just using your voice. The next step would be to reach your arm through the cot bars to rub/pat their back. This will often be enough to settle them down again before any slight wake-up escalates into being fully awake. Try and resist standing up to settle them as this may encourage your child to stand up to be near you. Once standing, they become increasingly more wakeful. This method can be very effective as you are able to intercept and reassure them very quickly before they are completely awake, which may not have been the case had you have been in a different room and only responding to the noise from a monitor.

SEATED SETTLING

Calm your baby in your arms so that they are relaxed, then put them in their cot in a sitting position with their feet at the end. In doing so, you are not only placing them in a safe sleep position but also making them feel more secure. With their feet touching the end they feel supported.

Try not to have too much eye contact and stand so you are behind or to the side of them, not in their direct line of view.

Pat or rub your baby's back gently and slowly (similar speed to a heartbeat) and, as your baby settles down, gently lower them into a lying down position. Always keep your baby's head and neck supported while in the seated position and support the back of their neck when you lower them to the lying down position.

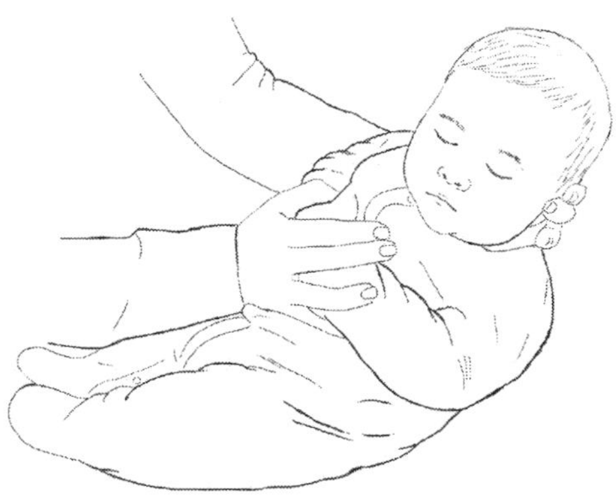

When they are lying down, slowly remove your hand, finger by finger, from the back of their neck. You may find it helpful to place your other hand on their chest.

If your baby wakes once you have taken your hands away, repeat the steps again. You may have placed them down prematurely.

SWADDLING

All babies are born with a startle reflex (Moro reflex). It has been found that the Moro reflex is generally present in a baby from weeks 25–30 of pregnancy[38]. It is involuntary, the infant's response to being startled, and it causes them to flail their arms and legs out, before reaching their arms to find their mother. Babies are only born with two fears: of falling and of loud noises. This is why a baby will often startle when you are placing them down in their cot or when they are drifting off to sleep and a noise startles them. The reflex usually disappears by the time a baby is six months old.

If they flail their arms in their sleep, they will very likely wake. Swaddling them prevents this. When swaddling, ensure that their hips aren't swaddled too tightly, and ensure that a light swaddle is used in warmer temperatures. A baby that can roll must NEVER be swaddled.

If your baby was born breech or has or had hip dysplasia, do not swaddle without it being okayed by your doctor.

SUCKING

Babies find sucking incredibly calming. This can be in the form of a feed, a dummy/pacifier or comfort toy. A comfort toy must not be left in the sleep space of a baby under the age of 12 months.

PATIENCE

Patience can sometimes be the greatest method for getting your baby to settle. All too often I work with families (and I have been guilty of this too) that go to their baby too quickly when they are showing signs such as grumbling, shouting or thrashing their arms and legs, thinking that they are not settling down, when in actual fact this is a baby's way of soothing themselves. Most babies will have a grumble for a few minutes before going to sleep. Allow them to do this. If you struggle with this, tell yourself that you will allow 30 seconds more than usual before tending to them and gradually, over a period of few days, stretch this time out. This is by no means a cry it out technique. When I say leave them to it, I mean if they are not distressed, not crying, but just having a moan. Many children will slam their legs up and down, which some parents find concerning, but it is actually a way of settling themselves.

SETTLING OLDER CHILDREN

Children who are of an age to understand words and can communicate verbally back to you often require different techniques to get them to sleep. Children are very clever and it is important to explain to them what is going on at every step and tell them what is coming next. A two-year-old child, for example, will understand, when you tell them they are having a bath and then it is bedtime, what is to come. When settling them down in their cot, explain to them that it is sleep-time and you will be back in the morning.

Reward games often work well with children over the age of two. A sticker reward chart usually goes down well as it is a visual goal for them to aim for. This can be very effective for children that like to get out of their bed in the night and come to the parental bed. They should never be punished for coming to you in the night, as they need to know they can if there is an issue or they feel unwell. However, by rewarding them for going back to bed quickly, you are giving them the message that they are to sleep in their own bed.

THE ALTERNATIVE BED POSITION

Sometimes, just moving the cot into a different position in the room can be enough to reset any bad habits, especially for children over twelve months who may be more mobile in their cot. This gives you the chance to start afresh, as your baby will have a different view of the room.

MY BIG GIRL/BOY BED

Toddlers love being able to make their own decisions and if you are having issues with your child leaving their bed in the night to be with you, consider taking them shopping and allowing them to pick some brand new bedcovers with a pretty pattern or a print of their favourite cartoon character. Have them try and help you make the bed up and, while making it, explain to them that now they have their big boy/girl bedcovers it means that they are old enough to stay in bed all night long with them.

ROOMING IN

Similar to the floor bed scenario with younger babies, sometimes toddlers go through phases of feeling unsettled. This can be due to so many things, such as starting nursery, a new baby coming, hormonal fluctuations or growth spurts that have an impact on night-time sleep. It may be that they just need extra reassurance from you during a few nights. You can set up a mattress in the room for three or four nights, so you can settle them before things escalate into a full wake up. I would recommend ensuring that you leave the room before they wake in the morning, which may mean setting a quiet vibrate alarm on your phone or asking your partner to wake you. Doing this ensures that your child doesn't become reliant on waking up to find you there every morning.

TRANSITIONING TO A BED FROM A COT

There is often a lot of anxiety around moving your toddler from their cot into a toddler bed. Generally, the main worry is their staying in the bed and settling down to sleep. With no restrictions on the sides, they are able to get out of bed when they like and their room will be a whole new area to investigate. Ensure that all furniture is secure and cannot be pulled over onto them and that stair gates are installed so that if they do walk out of their room in the night, they do not stumble down the stairs.

Involve your toddler in the process. Allow them to be present when you construct their bed and allow them to pick out their choice of bedding. Talk to them about the transition into their big bed in the days prior to making the change and talk about it in a positive manner, working up some excitement around it. During the day that you are going to make the transition, go into the room with your toddler and show them their bed. Talk to them about how it is their new bed and how grown-up they now are to have a big bed. On the night that you make the transition, keep your bedtime routine the same and keep the atmosphere as calm as possible. Try not to make too much of an issue of it. Tuck them up in bed and leave the room. You will probably find that they get out of bed out of curiosity a few times. Go back into the room, do not be cross with them and tell them to go back to bed. If you need to sit in the room for 5–10 minutes to reassure them, then do so.

If you find that they are uncomfortable with not being able to see anything when they get up and out of bed, consider using a red night light so that they can find their own way back to bed.

A reward chart can be very effective when transitioning to toddler beds and many children also respond very well to reading books about staying in bed.

Never punish a child for getting out of bed. Bed should always have a positive attitude surrounding it. Be firm and set boundaries, but getting angry – especially in the first few days – can be very counterproductive. A child should never go to bed upset.

CHILDREN'S STORIES FOR SLEEP

There are many fantastic books about sleep that you can read to your child to help them understand about bedtime. These work better from the age of about two years old and can help with slightly older children too. Some of my favourites are:

A Bed of your Own by Mij Kelly
My Big Boy Bed/My Big Girl Bed by Amanda Li
Your Own Big Bed by Rita Bergstein
Ten Minutes to Bed: Little Dinosaur by Rhiannon Fielding
I'm Not Sleepy: Helping Toddlers to Sleep by Campbell Books
Ten Little Night Stars by Deb Gruelle

SETTLING TO SLEEP AWAY FROM HOME

Sometimes it may be necessary for your child to sleep away from home, for example at a nursery. I get asked a lot about sleep at nursery as it can be quite different to how it is at home. I think it is important to have a conversation with the childcare setting about how they facilitate sleep and what they are happy to do to help encourage it when it is needed, but perhaps being resisted. My suggestion would be to help your child in their new environment by sending in familiar bedding (such as a cot sheet or sleep bag) from home that is not freshly washed and therefore smells of home. As previously mentioned, scent is very comforting for a baby. If you are breast feeding your baby, consider sending in a comforter that has been down mum's top for a while so that it has a comforting scent. Encourage the nursery staff to use a sleep bag at nap times if you do so at home and that they loosen any tight clothing, so that the child is as comfortable as possible.

Try not to get too stressed if your child is sleeping less at nursery than they do at home. This is very common. On the days that they are at home, allow them a little extra sleep at nap times if they want to, so that they can catch up on the sleep that they have missed when away from home. There is no point worrying about something that you do not have much control over. I find that during the first few weeks of starting nursery, children don't tend to sleep as well as they do at home, but after a few weeks when they have settled in, it generally improves.

Chapter 9

THE MOST COMMON SLEEP ISSUES

There are many issues that can arise when it comes to a baby's sleep patterns. I use the word "issue" loosely, as to some these patterns may pose no issue, while others, who perhaps have work commitments or other children to care for, may find they disrupt their own sleep pattern and make functioning properly very difficult. For example, if a baby is waking up early (pre-6am) this may be a huge issue for someone who is not a morning lark, but for others it will present no problem. I will talk through the most common "issues" that families approach me with, but bear in mind that it is only an issue if it is a problem for your baby, you, or your family dynamics.

You will find that many people have opinions on how your baby should or shouldn't sleep or how you should or shouldn't respond to their needs. Your baby's sleep and the way you approach it is nobody's business but yours, so take unsolicited advice with a pinch of salt.

SELF-SETTLING

The issue with self-settling is that only around 50% of babies are actually capable of being able to settle themselves. All too often I get asked how to teach a baby to do it. My response to this is usually to ask the same question of the parents. As adults, we have much more control over our emotions and are capable of feeding ourselves, visiting the toilet or changing our clothes if we are too hot or cold. A baby is not capable of doing these things. My point is that we need to ensure that all needs are properly met before we can even consider a baby's being able to settle themselves to sleep. The technique I use on page 161 (cot comfort) greatly improves a baby's ability to feel settled in their sleep space but it is our job as parents to provide emotional support for our children (filling up their happy tank) and ensuring they are offered sleep when it is needed.

I truly believe that being able to self-settle is developmental and is not something that a baby is actually capable of doing if they are in a stressed state due to emotional immaturity and reliance on their parents for basic needs. This will of course come in time, but children generally aren't able to begin to rationalise emotions until they are over two years old, and this is usually a learned behaviour from their parents. A two-year-old, in comparison with a twelve-month-old, will generally have some understanding when you reason with them. They will understand sequences of events far better and the consequences of certain behaviours. Before that, you'll have noticed changes happening progressively in a child. At the age of 10–13 months, they'll be showing an ability to settle themselves better than a three-month-old baby can.[40]

A common self-settling behaviour, which parents often view as worrisome and usually do not recognise as a sign of a baby calming themselves, is when a baby slams their legs up and down in the cot repeatedly when going off to sleep or even bangs their head continually on the cot. Of course, this can be anxiety inducing for a parent, but if the baby is only doing this at times of sleep, it is likely their way of settling themselves. To you it may be stressful, as you may worry about them hurting themselves, but to them it is a soothing behaviour. It does not need to be intercepted unless they are causing injury to themselves which would be quite unlikely. Around 20% of babies do this, and they will usually grow out of it by the time they are about 3 years old.

Sleep development phases

Although this is most commonly known as the sleep regression phases, I dislike the term. The definition of regression is "a return to a former or less developed state", but when babies reach significant sleep stages, they are never going backwards with their sleep state, they move forward into a more adult-like sleep state. This is why I like to call them sleep development phases.

More often than not, sleep disruptions are blamed on these phases. Google your sleep issue or ask a sleep question in a social media group and "sleep regression" will probably be the most common suggestion for what is causing the issue.

Baby suddenly won't sleep? SLEEP REGRESSION
Baby wakes early? SLEEP REGRESSION
Baby won't nap? SLEEP REGRESSION
Baby wakes all the time? SLEEP REGRESSION

Although I am not denying that sleep development phases happen, all too often a sleep issue is blamed on this when it it's actually something else which is causing it.

Also, not all babies will show signs that they are going through a sleep development phase, so don't start dreading these milestones. Some babies will not be phased by them at all, others may be unsettled for a couple of nights while they adjust, and a few may be affected for a few weeks. However, if you know how to handle it when it happens (and understand why it is happening) then it will allow you to put things in place to help you and your baby adjust to their new way of sleeping.

Sleep development phases generally happen around 4–6 months (more typically 4 months), 6–8 months (usually closer to 8 months), 18 months, and around 2 years.

You will notice that these periods generally coincide with a child hitting developmental milestones that seem to have a great effect on sleep.

4–6 months: rolling; melatonin production starting
6–8 months: up on all fours or beginning to crawl
18 months: most children walk by this point and also start being more verbal (speaking). Separation anxiety can also play a big part at this stage
2 years: bladder awareness; increased communication; possibly a new sibling coming along.

4-month sleep development phase

At the 4-month sleep development stage, the part of the baby's brain that produces melatonin is beginning to function, so a baby begins to understand the difference between night and day and also starts experiencing the lighter stages of sleep more (Stages 1 and 2). Because of this, around this age you will find that a baby may show the following signs:

- Suddenly only napping for short periods
- Frequent waking in the early part of the night
- Resisting naps
- Early waking

A quick fix that will generally help your baby is to assess whether they need to drop a nap if you start seeing any of the above issues (usually the shortest of the day, or instead of putting them straight back to bed after the first feed of the day, keep them up for an hour or so).

Always allow 3–4 consistent days of changes to see a potential improvement. Don't give up if, after one day of making a change, it makes no difference. This is normal.

It may be beneficial to use white or pink noise at nap times as they may be sensitive to noise if they're going through Stages 1 and 2 of sleep (light phases).

Go back to basics and reassess maximum wake time (see page 37).

6–8 month development phase

At around eight months, a lot is going on for your baby. They generally become more mobile, usually rolling around a bit. They also have growth spurts, so you may experience more frequent feeding. At this age, they have a better understanding of routines and sequences of events that happen in the day. Around this time you may notice that night-time sleep becomes disrupted and they have frequent wake-ups and may be more difficult to settle.

Due to being more awake and mobile during the day (and potentially wanting shorter naps) their sleep need may increase at night-time. This is a time where babies often transition from three naps to two (timed in the morning and afternoon) but if they have had a day full of stimulation or physical activity, a third nap may still be required. I would, however, recommend that if they need one (based on sleep cues) in the later part of the afternoon, it is not much longer than 30–50 minutes or one sleep cycle. (You can work out how long your baby's sleep cycle is by using the average duration for their shortest nap of the day – usually between 30 and 50 minutes.)

If they do not seem to require a third nap, consider bringing bedtime slightly earlier. An earlier bedtime does not necessarily mean an earlier wake time. Watch your baby's sleep cues in the evening to assess whether it might benefit them.

It is important to keep wake-up time consistent, and if they have had a severely disrupted night try not to allow them to overcompensate for the lack of sleep by lying in for longer in the morning as this will have a knock-on effect on naps and potentially create a repeat performance the following night.

18-month development phase

Around 18 months, most children are walking, climbing and in general their speech will suddenly take a bit of a leap. They may be stringing together a couple of words, and will have much more understanding of situations. They may show signs of a sleep development phase in the following ways:

- Becoming more clingy towards you
- Standing up for long periods of time in their cot at night
- Trying to climb out of their cot
- Pacing their cot
- Talking/babbling for up to an hour when they wake in the night

The majority of the time, these sleep changes happen because your baby is more aware of your not being present.

Allow plenty of time during the day playing games of peek-a boo which helps them understand that just because you cannot be seen, it doesn't mean you are not nearby. Also, if you go out of sight but are still in the house with them (eg. not leaving them with someone else and going away from them), ensure that you use your voice to reassure them that you are still nearby. You could carry on talking to them, tell them that you won't be long or try singing/whistling so that they know you are near. Never sneak out of a room, thinking that because you didn't tell them you were going, they will not get upset. It is important that they are aware of your actions and you communicate with them. And if you say that you will be right back, ensure that you do come right back. If you are leaving the house or leaving them with someone else for a time, make sure that you tell them. Babies understand a lot more than we think. If you are going to work, say: "I'm off to work and will be back later, and [relevant name] is going to be looking after you today. I promise I'll be back, you don't need to worry". Give them a cuddle and a kiss to reassure them. If you are settling them down to sleep, tell them that you will be back as soon as they wake up – and again, give them a cuddle and a kiss. Tell them that if they need you, you are nearby, but it is sleep time now and you will see them when you wake.

If your baby is playing midnight gymnastics in their cot, which is very common when they are trying to master a new skill, ensure that you practise their new skill lots with them during the day. Set up obstacle courses to help them with climbing, jumping and walking as this may reduce their practising at night. Try not to do it too close to bedtime though, as this may overstimulate them.

If there is lots of chatting going on in the night, have lots of conversation with them during the day. It is so common for children to reel off names of their family in the middle of the night or lists of animals! It is exciting for them as they are mastering a new way of communication. I have spent many a night listening to my children reeling off every member of the family over the monitor or practising animal sounds at 3am. It is developmental and there is nothing wrong if they are doing this. Leave them to it if they are not upset. Be proud that they are so excited with all that they are learning, because you helped to teach it to them.

2-year development phase

This phase is usually driven by emotions and manifests with the following issues.

- Frequent wakes at night
- Resistance to going down to sleep
- Seems full of energy at usual nap time
- Hyperactivity at bedtime
- Severe crying when you put them down at night (but not during the day)

So what causes these issues?

In general, the sleep development phase happens between two and three years of age and is very emotionally driven. We all know the saying "terrible twos", referring to the behaviour from a 2+ year old. Although it is very emotion driven, they do not understand how to control these emotions and this usually manifests in a tantrum! Next time you see a tantrum brewing, remember that your child doesn't know how to react to the sudden rush of hormones/emotions that take over them. You will see a toddler almost having a fight with them. A great description I heard, is that, "the Universe just isn't going their way."

My first recommendation is to talk to them. Talk them through sequences, talk about emotions and offer understanding. Fill up their happiness tank during the day, giving lots of emotional support, praising them, being physically affectionate with them, and in general making them know that they are very loved. By doing this you are ensuring that when they do go to bed they have a full happiness tank. A child who has a happiness tank running low will generally be more needing of you at night. If they are resisting going to bed and communicate that they want to be with mummy/daddy, talk to them about the sequences of events that are happening or going to happen. It is very important to remain consistent and for things to be predictable for a toddler. A slight change in routines or sequences before bed can throw them off course, cause confusion, and end up in meltdown!

What they say to you (may not be in these words)	Explain to them	Reasoning
I want to be with you	I am nearby but it is time for you to get some sleep now. When you wake up in the morning, we will do (activity)	Reassuring them that you are always near and after the sleep there is something planned
I don't want to go to bed	Mummy and daddy are going to bed soon as well. If you go to sleep, then in the morning we can have fun again	Explaining where you will be. Telling them what happens when they wake up
I'm not well/ something hurts	First ensure that they are well. But toddlers understand that when they are unwell they generally get more attention. Reassure them that they are ok and there is nothing to worry about. If they say something hurts, for example their finger, offer to kiss it better. If they were using this as an excuse not to go to bed, kissing their finger better may pacify them. This is a sign they are wanting reassurance	Acknowledging their concern and ensuring if they are unwell that their needs are met. They sometimes don't understand the phrase "I'm not well" but know that it brings attention, so this is essentially what they are craving. Meet that need, reassure them and tell them it is bedtime.

What they say to you (may not be in these words)	Explain to them	Reasoning
I want another story	Ensure that you have explained to them before the story that this is the one you are going to read tonight and they can pick another one for the next night. Allowing them to pick the bedtime story often helps. Ensure that in their room they only have the story/stories that are going to be read. If others can be seen, it may confuse them.	Toddlers often stall bedtime by requesting another story. By being clear before the story starts, they know what to expect.
I need the toilet	If you have a child of potty training age, you may need to take this "excuse" seriously as they may not want to wet or soil their nappy. But give them one chance rather than multiple chances to go. Tell them that you will take them to the toilet and then it is bedtime.	This could be a genuine request so allow them the chance to use the bathroom but set limits with how many times you will take them. This can be used as a good "excuse" not to go to bed

If they haven't dropped to one nap a day by this development phase then now will probably be the time. It will usually be the morning nap that they resist, so gradually reduce this in duration. If they are resisting it, allow them to have up to 30 minutes' rest time in their cot if they aren't crying. If, over a period of three days, they aren't napping at all during this time on any day then reduce the time in cot by 10 minutes per day, so that on day 4 they have no time in the cot at all. Because of the dropped morning nap, it is likely that you will need to bring the afternoon nap a bit earlier (towards the middle of the day). This nap will be around 1–2.5 hours. It shouldn't extend much beyond this or it may affect night-time sleep. It also shouldn't be within 4–5 hours of bedtime.

If they usually go to bed at 7pm and wake at 7am, the middle of the day would be around midday for a couple of hours. This is right around lunchtime so make the decision whether to do lunch before or after the nap. If you have a child that doesn't suffer from digestive discomfort, they may be quite happy sleeping on a full tummy. However, if you have a child who has allergies and intolerances, it may be worth holding off until after the nap for lunchtime and giving a light snack before they go down.

EARLY WAKING

"ANYTHING PAST 6AM FOR A BABY UNDER 12–18 MONTHS FALLS INTO THE RANGE OF NORMAL"

WHAT IS EARLY WAKING?

Firstly, when I talk about an early wake I mean when a baby wakes and is ready for the day, not those occasions when the baby wakes for a feed and goes back to sleep. With an early wake, they may be bouncing around ready to go, full of beans and will not settle back down again. They want to be out of their cot and up!

There are a lot of things that will contribute to what makes us feel that a time is "too early". Some families may accept 5am as being perfectly acceptable, as they themselves wake early for the day, but for the majority it may well feel like the middle of the night.

Anything past 6am for a baby under 12–18 months falls into the realms of normal. If you have no work commitments, I would encourage you to embrace this wake-up time (if after 6am) as it is very normal and not a huge lot can be done about it! You may need to adapt your own sleep patterns temporarily to suit your baby's wake-up time. However, if we are talking about a wake-up time that is before 6am and it starts having an impact on the way you function during the day, there are a few simple solutions that can help.

WHY DOES IT HAPPEN?

Babies' wake-up time is very much hormone-driven and light is a huge contributing factor to these hormones being produced. When the optical nerve senses light (which it can do even through closed eyes in the light phases of sleep), it sends a signal to the brain to produce cortisol which will start to wake the baby.

With very young babies, an early wake may be for a feed. If they are waking out of hunger then they will usually go straight back to sleep. The early wakes I am talking about here are not hunger wake-ups.

SIMPLE SOLUTIONS

Never underestimate how even the slightest bit of light can have a huge effect on when your baby wakes. As I spoke about earlier in the book, if you can, invest in blackout blinds and even curtains over the top if any light is creeping in around the edges. The room needs to be so dark that, when the lights are off and blinds or curtains are shut, you cannot see your hand in front of your face. Remember, babies are NOT born scared of the dark.

If blackout blinds or curtains are not an option due to cost, window film can be purchased which provides a completely dark environment. It can be removed easily and cut to size. This does however stay on the window until you remove it. Always check that any window film you apply is compatible with double or triple glazed windows due to the possibility of it causing overheating of the glass and a build-up of pressure which could damage the window.

A very simple solution I have used in the past is to tape down the sides of the blinds so that no light seeps in at all. Of course you have to be careful that this doesn't damage your paintwork or wallpaper and it may be easier just to keep the blind down permanently if you use this short-term solution.

If you need to have a light in the room for night-time feeds/changing/resettling, use a red night light so that it doesn't interfere with melatonin production.

Another reason for a very early wake-up call is if the baby feels cold. Body temperature dips between the hours of 2 and 5am and is also the time when the house is coolest. Due to feet being the first part of the body to feel cold (even if the baby is still warm), this can often cause a wake up. Put socks on your baby if the room temperature does significantly change by a few degrees in the early hours and this should help prevent it. This can be beneficial to children of any age. In warmer months, when room temperatures are naturally warmer, this should not be necessary.

An overfilled nappy can also cause a wake up. This doesn't affect younger babies so much, as the volume of urine is much less, but as babies drink more milk their nappies can get very heavy after many hours. Size up on the night-time nappy (provided that it doesn't cause a leak if it's too big!) for greater absorbency. It may allow them to stay in a settled sleep for a couple more hours. A nappy with an elasticated waist can be beneficial too, as it will adapt depending on how full or empty the bladder is, unlike a traditional nappy that is done up at a certain tightness.

Some babies produce lots of urine at night-time and this can lead to a leaking nappy, which in turn makes them feel uncomfortable. If sizing up on the nappy doesn't help, ensure that any clothing isn't too tight around the nappy area. If your baby wears a vest that does up around the nappy area, when the nappy fills, the vest will become tighter around the nappy and becomes another absorbent layer to get wet. Try a bigger vest if that is the case.

Very similar to light, noise can also interrupt a baby's sleep. As you are now aware, every human goes through phases of light sleep and deep sleep for many cycles a night. When we go into the lightest phase of sleep (NREM 1&2), if there is noise a baby may wake up. Some contributing sounds which may wake babies in the early hours:

- Birds singing in the summer months from 4am
- Somebody in the household having a very early alarm
- Somebody in the household getting in from a night shift and making light noise
- An adjoining neighbour's alarm going off
- The adjoining house making noise if they get up very early
- Traffic starting up on a nearby road
- A boiler firing up and radiators coming on, making clicking noises as they heat (check your thermostat to ensure the timer is changed)
- Another child in the house or same room waking
- Someone in the house getting up in the night
- The mother pumping milk at night (if not feeding overnight but still pumping)

As silly as some of these may sound, these are all examples of noises that have woken babies I have worked with where the families hadn't even considered them to be the cause.

If you do have a baby that is very sensitive to sound, using white noise or pink noise overnight can be helpful.

IF THE SIMPLE SOLUTIONS DON'T WORK

Another reason could be that they have just had enough sleep. Society tells us that babies "should" sleep 12 hours per night. Modern society has conditioned us to have goals of babies sleeping 7 to 7. Unfortunately this is often unrealistic as the majority of babies are incapable of sleeping for this long stretch (even with wake-ups during the night-time sleep period). A more realistic expectation may be 10–11 hours, and even those may be fragmented. If you do not have a "12-hour night baby" then consider adjusting bedtime. For example, if you currently put them to bed at 7pm and they are waking at 5am every morning then you may have a baby who is just not capable yet of sleeping for more than 10 hours at night. This will come in time, but often doesn't until around 18 months for most babies. Although we often want to have our evenings to ourselves, we may have to make the compromise of putting our baby to bed a little later to encourage a later wake time in the morning. If your baby is having naps that are appropriate for their age (see page 79) and they are still having early starts, adjust the bedtime so that it is later. I know this may not be what you want to read, but I have to be honest and give you realistic expectations.

To totally contradict this, a small percentage of babies actually need to go to bed a lot earlier than the time we are putting them to bed, but parents fear doing this as they worry that the wake time will become earlier. This should not be the case if your baby is having slightly less sleep at naps during the day than is recommended for them. An overtired child, due to lack of quality naps in the day, may wake up a couple of hours after putting them down to sleep, in which case I recommend putting them down to bed a bit earlier at night.

Tweak bedtime to see what works best for your child. Be consistent with the time change for a few days. It usually takes 3–4 nights to see a change in their sleep patterns when bedtime is adjusted.

Break the cycle

Sometimes we can go too quickly to a baby. We need to allow them some time to drop off back to sleep. They may have woken from a noise or a temperature change but are perfectly capable of getting themselves back to sleep. If we go to them too quickly it teaches them that they need us every single time to get back to sleep. Obviously if they are upset, go to them, but if they are chatting to themselves, rolling around, or just lying there awake, then leave them. They will cry out for you if you are needed.

Unnecessary feeding

Feeding is a very natural way to get a baby to relax and often fall back to sleep. However, if they have been well fed throughout the day and night, I would advise only giving a small feed on those post-4am wakes if this is your method of getting them back to sleep (for babies over 6 months only). If bottle feeding, giving a huge volume of milk in the early hours can actually be counterproductive as their stomach will become used to the large volume and it soon becomes a habit. By giving just a couple of ounces of milk or a breastfeed that may be shorter in duration than usual, it quenches any thirst and satisfies hunger but doesn't lead to them rejecting their milk at normal wake-up time.

SHORT NAPS

A nap is a sleep cycle or a series of sleep cycles linked together. It is actually fairly easy to work out how long your baby's sleep cycle is. To work this out, over the period of three days, take note of how long each of their naps are. Some may be around 30 minutes, some up to a couple of hours. Make note of all of the naps (that are over 25 minutes). It may be something like this (example of a 5-month-old)

Day 1

Nap 1	31 minutes
Nap 2	60 minutes
Nap 3	34 minutes
Nap 4	33 minutes

Day 2

Nap 1	64 minutes
Nap 2	90 minutes
Nap 3	35 minutes
Nap 4	29 minutes

Day 3

Nap 1	28 minutes
Nap 2	68 minutes
Nap 3	31 minutes
Nap 4	35 minutes

The shorter naps (all around 30 minutes) are a single sleep cycle, most likely. This baby has an average sleep cycle of about 29–35 minutes. If you average that out, then the sleep cycle is about 32 minutes. On day 1 at nap 2 they slept for almost double this, so that would be two sleep cycles. On day 2 at nap 2, they slept for 90 minutes, so that would be three sleep cycles.

If your baby is only ever having short naps (rarely getting to more than one sleep cycle), it suggests that they are having issues of linking their cycles together. Some children are perfectly fine just having a few short naps during the day, but for others it can have an impact on mood and night-time sleep.

A baby's sleep cycle will vary between 30 and 50 minutes, so please assess how long your baby's sleep cycle is before starting the exercise. For the purpose of this exercise, I am going to use the same baby that I have used in the example who has a sleep cycle of approximately 32 minutes.

Go to your baby 5 minutes before the end of their usual sleep cycle. So with this baby, I will go to them at 27 minutes and be nearby, ready for them to stir. Look out for signs such as their breathing rate increasing, light twitching, making quiet noises or moving. When this happens, place your hand on your baby's chest and apply a light pressure, using your voice to shush and reassure them. You may need to do this for a few minutes until their breathing slows again and they go into the next sleep cycle. Keep as quiet as you can (apart from using your voice to gently soothe them.)

Don't feel disheartened if this is not successful the first few times you do it, you will learn to recognise when they need resettling. If they do wake up completely, don't stress yourself out, but try again on the next nap.

Aim to start this when you know that for a couple of days you can really focus on it without interruptions. Don't let it rule your life, though, or feel that you have to do it for every nap of the day.

Top tips:

Have the room as dark as possible
Have the room as quiet as possible

Focus on getting your baby down for a nap at the right time by watching their sleep cues (see page 32). By getting them down for a nap at the right time when they are not overtired or under-tired, it will encourage a better quality sleep. If a baby is put down too overtired, they will crash into deep sleep too quickly (Stages 3&4), meaning they miss NREM 1&2 so the sleep cycle will be shorter than usual.

Ensure a clean nappy is put on about 20 minutes before their usual nap time so that you don't need to do a nappy change right before their nap, which can make them become more alert.

If you're aiming for a nice long sleep then carry out a mini bedtime routine (of only a couple of minutes) so perhaps a quick story or a mini massage to help calm them.

Avoid toys with loud noises and flashing lights too close to a nap time so they are not over stimulated.

If you use white noise/pink noise at night then use it for a nap too.

Put your baby in their sleep bag if you usually use one at night but remember to remove any tight clothing so they are comfortable.

REFUSAL OF NAPS

A complete refusal of naps is generally a sign that the ideal nap time has been missed or they are not tired enough yet.

Do the checklist.

Are they fed?
Are they too cold?
Are they too hot?
Are they irritated by any clothing?
Have they been winded?
Are they unwell?
Is their happy tank full?

If any of these need addressing, then do so, as they may prevent a nap from happening if the need is not met.

One of the other main causes of refusal of a nap is when a baby is ready to drop a nap for the day. This usually happens around 4 months, 6–8 months, 12–18 months and 2–3 years old.

Signs that a baby may be ready to drop a nap:

- Becoming more difficult to settle at their usual time
- Only napping for 15–20 minutes
- Taking over 20 minutes to settle for the nap and not protesting during this time (just lying there wide awake)
- Night-time sleep suddenly becoming more disrupted

If this is the case, try and remove that nap and see how your baby fares. It may mean having to readjust the other nap timings for the day by shifting them a little bit earlier or later, depending on which nap they want to drop. For the first couple of weeks you will likely find that some days they still need the nap and some they don't. It really depends on activity levels. If you remove it every day (when some days they may still need it) you may find this causes night-time disruption.

Go with the flow and let them lead you. Don't get stressed if they refuse the nap, it may just be an adjustment to dropping it entirely.

An example schedule of a dropped nap for a baby around 6 months may look something like this:

Nap 1	8am
Nap 2	11.30am
Nap 3	2.30pm
Nap 4	4.30pm (The nap they may drop)

TO....

Nap 1	8.30am
Nap 2	12pm
Nap 3	3.30pm

You can see that the naps have shifted a little later, allowing for the time between wake up from the last nap and bedtime to be a little longer, yet the baby still being well rested throughout the day. The fourth nap is generally a short "catnap" which helps link the time between the third nap and bedtime, but as their maximum wake time extends, if the fourth nap is still present, they will be too awake and not enough sleep pressure will have been built up for bedtime – they may go down at their usual bedtime but may wake frequently. In effect, they are treating their bedtime as a nap and not their night-time sleep, which will be a longer stretch.

FREQUENT NIGHT WAKES (PRE-MIDNIGHT)

There are various things that can cause wake-ups shortly after putting a baby to bed.

OVERTIRED

One of the main causes of frequent wake-ups in the earlier part of the night is that the baby is overtired. When that is the case, they don't fall gently into sleep: they skip very quickly through stages 1 and 2 of sleep. Because of this they generally wake after one or two sleep cycles (after 30–60 minutes). If you feel that they have not napped well during the day, reassess their maximum wake times and focus on a few days of really good quality naps (at home, ideally in a quiet environment) to get them back on track. Ensure that the last nap of the day is not too close to bedtime but also not too far away. You can do this by working out their maximum wake time. If, for example, their maximum wake time is three hours, ensure your baby is in bed ready to sleep around three hours from waking from their last nap. Sleep definitely promotes sleep, and a well-rested baby will sleep better at night-time.

"SLEEP PROMOTES SLEEP AND A WELL RESTED BABY WILL SLEEP BETTER AT NIGHT-TIME."

NOT TIRED ENOUGH

Putting a baby to bed too early (before their maximum wake time) may see them treat the sleep like a nap. Sleep pressure needs to build throughout the day, so if you are experiencing frequent wakes soon after putting them to bed, check to see if the total nap time they are having in the day is a little too much. If it is, reduce one of the naps by one sleep cycle.

Try and rouse a baby after a complete sleep cycle (30–50 minutes) as waking them before this may mean they are cranky from being woken from a deep sleep.

BODY TEMPERATURE

Children under two years of age, in particular, can struggle to sleep if their body temperature isn't back to normal at bedtime. Children under two cannot regulate their own body temperature – as the part of their brain that regulates it isn't mature enough – so it is important that we help them with this. Influences on body temperature might include:

Being outside during the afternoon in cold weather

Ensure they are dressed appropriately in layers that can be removed if they get too warm from physical activity. Put a hat on your baby if out walking in cold weather so that heat doesn't escape from their head. Hands and feet are a poor indicator of body temperature, but feel the back of their neck for a reasonably reliable representation of how warm they are. Ensure they are fed if you are out and about for long periods of time. The body needs to burn calories to create heat so a hungry baby will not have the energy to keep warm.

Being too hot, from lots of physical activity

Physical activity is great for health, however it may take the under-twos up to a couple of hours to get their body temperature back to normal. Try and avoid too much physical activity in the two hours before bedtime.

Eating spicy food

In general, hot, spicy foods are stimulants and increase body temperature. This may only be by a very small amount, but if your baby is having frequent wakes after bedtime, then consider not giving them spicy foods for their last meal.

Nightwear that is too thick

If you dress your baby in layers in colder months, it is easy to remove a layer at a time if they get too hot. If they have a vest under a babygrow, for example, you can just remove the babygrow if they get too warm. Blankets or sleep bags may not be necessary in warmer months and, if using a blanket, then a cellular one won't heat your baby as much as a normal blanket may.

Not enough clothing so they feel cold

Do not rely on hands or feet as an indicator of body temperature, feel the back of their neck or chest. It may be as simple as having a vest under a baby grow, but one of my favourite quick fixes for babies waking frequently in the night during the colder months is to pop a pair of socks on them (even under a babygrow).

Baths

Baths can significantly change the body's core temperature. The ideal water temperature is between 36C and 38C. There are various thermometers that can be purchased to check the temperature. If you do not have one, use your elbow or inside of your wrist to test the temperature. The water should feel warm and not hot. Babies cannot tolerate a bath as warm as an adult tends to prefer. Baby skin is very sensitive and they do not need bathing every day (a wipe down every day is a must though!).

If the bath temperature is even a degree too cool or warm, it can take up to a couple of hours for the baby to get their temperature back to normal again. This can cause interruption to their sleep. If you find that your baby is very irritated after a bath due to going from the warm bath to a cooler room, ensure that you have towels ready for them and that they are well wrapped up and dried totally before moving to the room. Some babies will cry after a bath, often due to the significant temperature change, so consider a different bath-time, one that isn't close to bedtime. I would recommend avoiding a bath within the hour before bedtime so that it allows them time to get body temperature back to normal. Warming towels often really helps soothe a baby, so they go straight into a nice warm towel to be dried.

Illness

Illness can be a significant cause to changes in body temperature. With high fevers come sleep disruption and upset. If a child has a high temperature then a bath that is a degree or so cooler than normal (around 34–36C) may bring their temperature down a degree or so which may make your child feel better.

Offer plenty of fluids to your baby. If you are not getting six to eight wet nappies a day from your baby while they are unwell, consult your doctor. If at any point your baby's fontanelle (soft spot on their head) starts to sink, you must seek medical attention immediately as this is a sign of dehydration.

If their temperature is not reducing, even when using infant paracetamol, speak to your doctor.

If you are unwell too and are breastfeeding your baby, carry on breastfeeding if you can, as you will pass antibodies on to your baby to help fight the illness.

FREQUENT NIGHT WAKES (ALL NIGHT)

As you now know, night waking is normal. However, if it is very regular and your baby is not having stretches of sleep for longer than an hour or so then this would be classed as frequent night wakes. There are generally only a handful of causes for very frequent waking in the night.

The first is that daytime naps are causing disruption. Based on the recommended nap needs for your baby's age, check to see if your schedule is significantly different, then go back to basics assessing their sleep cues to see if they are being put down to sleep too early or late for naps. If they are only having short naps in the day, work on extending them and this should see an improvement in the night-time sleep. (See page 142.)

The other cause of frequent wake-ups (not hunger) could be some sort of digestive discomfort caused by trapped gas or food that is digesting slowly. Ensure that your baby is very well winded before any sleep. Trapped gas can be extremely uncomfortable, and even painful. Until a baby is around 4–9 months of age, they are unable to bring up the trapped wind themselves. I find that many parents stop winding their babies as soon as they start to burp independently. However, it is important to continue to wind them until around 12 months of age as, although they may be able to bring some wind up, it is important to ensure that it has all come up. Then, when you lay them down, it doesn't cause pain or discomfort.

After a feed (even with breastfed babies, who don't tend to take in as much air as a bottle-fed baby), spend time winding your baby until they bring the air up (or down!). See pages 59 and 60 for winding techniques in detail.

FOOD DISCOMFORT

> "BE MINDFUL OF GIVING FOOD TO A BABY TOO SOON IN THE HOPE THAT IT WILL MAKE THEM SLEEP BETTER. MOST OF THE TIME IT WILL NOT."

Milk is the main source of nutrition for a baby until they are twelve months old. Unless you have been guided by a doctor, the recommended age to wean a baby (introducing food into their diet) is from six months. I see many sleep issues that have been caused from foods being introduced too soon or too quickly, so be mindful of giving food to a baby before the recommended age in the hope that it will make them sleep better. Most of the time it will not.

NEVER add products such as baby rice or porridge to a bottle as it is a choking hazard. They also have very little nutritional value.

When starting food with a baby, ensure that you try one type of food at a time and try it for about three days before introducing another type of food. This is to ensure that if your baby does have an allergic reaction you can quickly identify what has caused it.

It is a good idea to keep a food diary for babies that have regular night wakes after weaning commences. I find that often the wakes can be caused by something they are eating. This does not necessarily mean that they are allergic, it may just mean that they struggle to digest it. Some foods can cause a significant increase of gut bacteria, which is not a bad thing, but these bacteria produce more gas and, in turn, cause discomfort if the gas doesn't go up or down.

THE SPLIT NIGHT

It's party time! But not party time for anyone in your house apart from your baby. A split night is where a baby wakes after a few hours of being asleep and is ready to party. Literally.

They may stay awake for a couple of hours, they're rarely distressed and you may see them dancing about in their cot as if it is morning time. There is very little you can do to get them back to sleep as they are ready to be up!

A split night is generally caused by a body clock that is out of sync and a baby that is very overtired. They will often not be having enough quality sleep in the day (or be sleep-deprived from the night before) and then, when they are put down to bed, they treat it as a nap. Let's say they go down to bed at 7pm. As they're so exhausted, they may have a good 3.5–4 hour sleep and then they wake. Except as their body clock is so out of sync they treat this long sleep as a nap so are ready to go for a few hours as they would during the day! I'm sure it will make sense to a lot of you – a lightbulb moment as you read this.

(Please note: split nights are not applicable for babies under six months old, as it may be a sign that their melatonin production hasn't stabilised just yet. This isn't a true split night scenario.)

So, how do we tackle this?

This one takes perseverance and consistency. For about three days and nights, set aside a time when they are not at nursery and you do not have a very busy day the next day (in case you are very tired from their night-time party antics). Perhaps a weekend might be good.

When they are having a split night, it can easily be recognised as they will not be upset when they wake (though they may be upset for a minute or so upon waking). They may be bouncing about in their cot, singing, talking away or shouting for you. It will very much resemble behaviour that they usually display when waking from a daytime nap.

There is no point having a battle with them to get them to sleep. Keep them calm, keep lights dim, and keep them in their room. Taking them to another room may become habitual and start an even more complex issue. Either let them stay in their cot, singing and dancing for up to a couple of hours, or if that makes you feel uncomfortable, be with them in their room but keep the lights off. Attempts to get them to sleep will be quite futile. You may be able to relax them in your arms but I can pretty much guarantee that if you lay them down to sleep again, they will wake again, and be wide awake. Be reassured that this issue will not last long if tackled correctly.

THE PLAN

Start the morning after you have had a split night. DO NOT let them sleep later than around 6.30/7am. You do not want them to catch up on missed sleep from the night before (sorry, yes this is going to be tiring for you, but keep at it).

Use the nap guide below for the days after you have had the split night. It is really important that you encourage the naps as this is what is affecting the night waking. They are not necessarily waking because they are having too much sleep.

It is so important that you do not let them have excessively long naps after a split night.

6–12 months: 2–3 naps of no longer than 3 hours in total. But they must have at least 2 naps, so don't allow the first nap to be 3 hours as there will be no nap allowance left for the next. If the first nap is 2 hours, cap the second nap at 1 hour.

12–18 months: 2 naps, totalling no longer than 2.5–3 hours in total (mid-morning and early afternoon).

18 months or over: 1 nap, no longer than 2 hours and 15 minutes. It is very important for a baby this age to have a sleep in the day if you are experiencing split nights. This nap ideally needs to fall in the middle of the day. If you cannot get them to have more than a 1-hour sleep, attempt a very short nap (no longer than 45 minutes) mid-morning, and a nap just after lunchtime (no longer than 1.5 hours if they had a morning nap).

3 years or over: offer a quick power nap in the middle of the day, no longer than 1 hour in duration.

BEDTIME

Keep bedtime at their usual time, do not adjust it. In the 1.5 hours before bedtime, you must ensure that the environment is as calm as possible, lights are dim and no high energy activities take place. A relaxing bath may be a good start (1.5 hours before bedtime), then a massage, some milk and reading time. If it is still light outside, close curtains or blinds to ensure that the dimly lit environment starts the production of melatonin.

COMFORT

It is really important to cover every base that may rouse your baby around their usual "party time".

Cover this checklist:

Clean nappy

For slightly older children, or bottle-fed babies that are having very large volumes of milk before bed (7 ounces plus), try not to have that feed within 1 hour of bedtime to allow them time to empty their bladder after the milk, ready for a fresh nappy once they have done so. Consider using a pull-up nappy, which has an elasticated waist so will adapt to how full their bladder is (and won't become loose when emptied) and ensure that any vest that they may be wearing is not too tight around the nappy area to allow room for the expanding nappy.

Labels out of clothing

Remove any labels in their bedtime clothing that may be uncomfortable for them.

Dress them appropriately

Ensure that they are dressed appropriately and if it is cool in the house, consider an extra layer underneath their baby grow such as a vest and perhaps a pair of socks if the heating usually goes off around the time you go to bed (which is usually around the time your baby will begin to rouse if on a split night pattern).

A full tummy

For a child that is over 2 years of age, a split night can also be caused by a need for increased calories. A piece of toast before bed or a small snack can be helpful.

HOW LONG WILL THIS TAKE?

This will take a minimum of 3–4 nights of persistence as it takes a while for their body clock to adjust. Yes some babies may correct themselves after 1 day/night but these will be the minority. Remember to keep their wake time consistent. Do not let them catch up on sleep from disturbed sleep at night by having a super-long morning nap as they may very quickly slip back into a split night situation.

Is there a quick fix?

Well, maybe! It will work for a small percentage of children and there is no harm in trying this first before you try the 3–4 day plan. However, this way may not stick permanently – just a quick fix to give you a night or two of better sleep so you can catch up on sleep and prepare yourself for the 3–4 day plan.

QUICK FIX PLAN
THE RESET TECHNIQUE

This is by no means easy, but can often be very effective. Be aware, it can cause them to wake frequently on the night that you do it but it works by adjusting the out of sync body clock.

Do your normal bedtime routine.

Feed them away from the bedroom in a well-lit room at their normal time.

Keep them up until 2 hours past their normal bedtime. Do everything you can to keep them awake.

By this time they will be exhausted, so put them down to sleep.

VERY IMPORTANT You must ensure that they do NOT sleep past 6.30am/7am the next morning, as by keeping them up late, you are resetting their internal body clocks.

The next night, have normal bedtime and ensure that they don't nap more than they do usually during the day, or for longer than usual, as this will undo the work of the late-night bedtime the previous night.

TAKES A LONG TIME TO SETTLE

When settling a baby to sleep, we need to understand what is normal and what may be out of the normal range.

In general, if a baby takes over 20/25 minutes to fall asleep and there is lots of crying and resistance, it could be a sign that they are overtired and the sleep cues have been missed.

Spend a few days watching really carefully for sleep cues and see whether bedtime may need to brought a little bit earlier so that when you try to settle them they are calmer.

However, if they are taking this amount of time and are lying in their cot quite content, they may not have been ready for sleep just yet. It is actually quite healthy to allow a baby to have time in their cot on their own, even if not asleep. They will still be resting if they are calm.

You can use this table as a guide to judge how over/under tired your baby may be. Be aware, though, that if your baby falls asleep very quickly, yet they sleep very well at night and don't seem overtired during the day, it may just be the way they're wired, and shouldn't be viewed as an issue.

Time to fall asleep	State	Suggestion
Less than 5 minutes	Overtired	Assess whether they need an additional nap in the day or earlier bedtime
5–10 Minutes	Lower range of normal	May suggest baby is slightly overtired. Nothing to be concerned about, but if causing night wakes, focus on quality naps for a couple of days in quiet environments
10–20 Minutes	Normal	Optimum time to fall asleep
20 Minutes and distressed	Overtired	Try bedtime an hour earlier if naps cannot be optimised
20 Minutes and calm	Not tired enough	Try bedtime 30 minutes later but if you are not concerned about them lying there calmly, leave them. Quiet time is restful time too.

WILL ONLY BE ROCKED TO SLEEP

Rocking a baby can be a hugely successful method of settling a baby to sleep. They feel secure, are calmed by being close to you, and the motion relaxes them. If this is no problem for you, then don't let other people tell you it is an issue if you are comfortable with doing it every time for your baby.

As your baby grows and becomes heavier, it may however begin to become more difficult and tiring for you, mainly due to the fact that holding and rocking them in the middle of the night when you are extremely tired can become physically exhausting.

As rocking is generally a sleep association, my best method to reduce the need for rocking is to do my "overlap associations" approach. This is where you introduce a couple of new sleep associations for your baby, whilst still carrying out the rocking, so that they begin to associate the new technique and rely less on the rocking as you reduce it. If you were to just stop rocking them, when rocking was the only way they knew how to fall asleep, you will likely have a very upset and grumpy baby on your hands who resists sleep.

I find that the best way to reduce (or totally stop) the rocking is to gradually do my overlap technique over a 10–14 day period. This is a very gentle method for your baby and is much more likely to work long-term.

Pick a NEW sleep association (must not be something you currently use) from the following list:

- White noise or pink noise
- Using your voice to shush your baby
- A song or lullaby (or a sequence of a few that last around 10–15 minutes or can be played on a loop)
- Patting their back/bum
- A comforter (must be taken away once asleep if under 12 months old)
- Swaddling (only if they cannot yet roll)

THE PLAN

Bear in mind that if multiple people settle your baby to sleep and your baby relies on rocking from all of them, they must all do the same thing.

Step 1: Days 1–5

When settling your baby for a sleep, carry on rocking as you have been but use the sleep association that you have picked at the same time. Do this at the same time as rocking them EVERY, SINGLE TIME.

Step 2: Days 6–9

Continue using the same new sleep association every time you settle your baby but slow the rocking down day by day so that by day 10 you are able to hold your baby in a firm, still hold while you use the new sleep association.

Step 3: Days 10–14

Day by day, reduce how firmly you hold your baby so that by day 14 you can just hold them gently in your arms while still using the new association.

By this point, you should now be able to put your baby down in their bed. If you have chosen to pat your baby when you put them down, carry on patting for a minute or two (slowly) while they fall into a light sleep.

If you are using a sound, then you can gradually phase this out so it becomes quieter, until they are fast asleep and the noise can then be off.

If they wake and need settling, do not get them out of the cot, but use the new sleep association to settle them (eg. turn the white noise back on for 10 minutes until they resettle).

If you find that they don't adapt well when going to the next step, continue with the current step for a couple more days. Don't be afraid to take a step back if you feel it is too fast for them. Try not to skip forward through the steps too quickly though, as it may take you back to step 1 very quickly.

WILL ONLY BE FED TO SLEEP

Feeding to sleep is natural, and is nature's way of being able to satisfy hunger, or to comfort and settle a baby. So many parents use this as a very successful method to settle their baby to sleep. It doesn't need to be breastfeeding your baby to sleep either. You may choose to combination feed your baby, feed expressed breast milk or formula. Whichever method you use, it will bring comfort to your baby. You can still hold your baby close if bottle feeding them.

However, there may be times when it is unmanageable or becomes unmanageable. For example, if you are breastfeeding and need to be away from your baby or if your baby is experiencing frequent wake-ups and will only be resettled by latching on for a feed or requiring a couple of ounces of milk. If you are having to offer many feeds in the night it might begin to cause severe issues with your own sleep so that it becomes unmanageable.

Be aware that young babies do feed regularly throughout the night, and at certain stages you may find that they go through a phase of a few days where it seems to be that they are continually feeding in the night. This is usually down to a growth spurt and tends to settle down after two to three days.

I would not ever recommend night weaning before a child is weaned onto food and having established meals during the day to ensure they get plenty of calories. A lot of babies and toddlers will still want a feed during the night until around 18 months of age. This is normal. Some will still feed during the night even after this age. A very small percentage of babies, decide for themselves quite early on that they do not want to wake up for a feed. If this is the case, let them sleep. You do not need to wake them, unless it causes growth to slow or a health professional has advised you to wake them in the night for feeds for a medical reason.

The step-by-step plan will help ease away from feeding your baby to sleep yet still keep your baby settled and content. Doing this slowly also allows for milk supply (if breastfeeding) to adjust slowly and cause the least stress for your baby and reduce the risk of painful engorgement for the mother.

Breast milk is produced very much on a supply and demand basis so if you are very regularly feeding to sleep throughout the night, even if only very short or small feeds, then milk production will adjust so that the correct amount is available for your baby. If you suddenly remove the option of feeding to sleep, and it is something that you have done a lot throughout the night previously, you will likely find that for a few days you have engorgement. Breast milk will continue to be produced as if you were feeding regularly throughout the night. By reducing it slowly, the milk supply will adjust gradually.

BREASTFED BABY PLAN

Days 1–4

Feed your baby to sleep as normal but introduce a sound or song playing at the same time when you feed for EVERY SINGLE FEED.

If you are not keen on a sound being used, consider using a comforter toy that you can encourage the baby to hold when you are feeding. If you do choose to use one, put some breast milk on the toy an hour or so before a feed or put it inside your bra for a few hours so that it smells of your milk. Stroke your baby's nose with the comforter while feeding.

If your baby is under 12 months old, the comforter must not be left with them when they are put down to sleep.

Days 5–8

Continue using the sound/comforter when feeding but remove your baby from the breast before the end of a feed (try and reduce the feed by a minute). As you are probably aware, at the end of a feed a baby starts to flutter suck (see diagram) so when you feel them doing this remove them from the breast by placing a finger in their mouth to unlatch them. If they are unhappy about this, place your finger so that the top of it is near their bottom lip and your finger runs vertically down their chin. Keep this in place for a minute or so. This makes them feel like they are still close to you but keeps them in a calm state. (Instead of just removing them from you, which may make them root for more milk.)

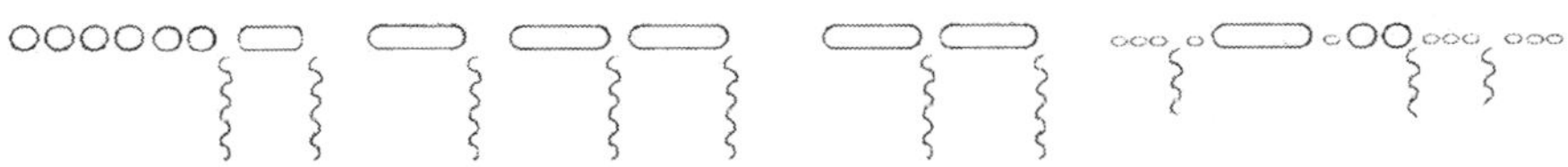

At the beginning of a feed, the sucking may be short and rapid

During the active feeding phase, the sucking may feel longer and more rhythmic with pauses for swallowing

Towards the end of a feed, your baby may start flutter sucking. This is where they suck lightly without many swallows and may fall asleep on the breast

Days 9–12

On days 9 to 12 concentrate on not having milk feed times within 15–20 minutes of any daytime nap. Settle them by first holding them (while having the new sound play or their comforter in hand) and then place them in their cot when awake, but sleepy. If you have caught them at exactly the right time (by looking out for sleep cues), they shouldn't cry.

They may moan a little which is fine, but allow them to do this for a few minutes. There is a difference between moaning themselves to sleep and crying, which you will see very clearly as if they're crying there will be tears. Feeding to sleep should now have been replaced with some of the new sleep associations.

WILL NOT GO IN THEIR COT

Resistance to going down to sleep in a cot is very common. Babies love nothing more than to be held, as it is warm, feels safe, and is very comforting.

A very common reason for being uncomfortable in their cot is a transition that is too quick from being in arms to being put down flat in it. Lying horizontal on a flat, firm surface feels very different to being in arms, especially for a baby who still has a strong startle reflex and wakes frequently because of this (see page 124).

From day one, the cot needs to feel like a calm and happy place to be. An empty cot is the safest kind of cot so don't be tempted to add in any soft toys, cot bumpers, sleep cocoons, duvets or pillows. A baby only requires warmth (from clothing and a sleep sack/swaddle) and nothing else apart from a dummy if you choose to use one, as this poses no risk to a baby.

Newborn cuddles really are the best and there is absolutely nothing wrong with having them sleep in your arms, but try and not have this for every sleep. That way, they will be comfortable being in their cot as well. The older they get, the more difficult sleeping in your arms may become (due to their weight) and also it gives you no time at all for yourself. Remember it is important for you to rest too.

In the first couple of weeks, where they will likely be sleeping on and off fairly constantly, try and have at least two to three naps in their own sleep space instead of on you or out in the pram. This gets them accustomed to their cot and makes them feel more comfortable about settling to sleep without being held. Have them in the same room as you, though, for all naps and sleeps, as per safe sleep guidelines. This doesn't mean that you cannot pop out of the room for a few moments, but ensure that if you do so their sleep space is safe and cannot be interfered with by young siblings or pets.

Ideally, have the room as dimly lit as possible for their naps. I am a firm believer in the interference of too much light causing shorter nap times during the day, and as it is difficult to tell when melatonin starts to be produced, there is no harm to have the nap times dimly lit from day one.

If you have got to the point where your baby will not sleep anywhere but on you, you could try using a sling to give yourself a bit more freedom. Slings are a great way of being able to keep your baby close to you so they feel secure, yet you can also do things around the house as your hands are free. As mentioned earlier, try not to have every sleep using a sling as it is important for a baby to get used to their sleep space (cot/Moses basket etc.).

Follow the next plan to help your baby be more comfortable with their cot. The plan is only to be carried out during the day when you are present, as it might involve the baby having a toy in the cot with them.

"GOING TO BED OR TO THEIR BEDROOM MUST NEVER BE A PUNISHMENT"

THE PLAN

THE COT COMFORT EXERCISE

This teaches your baby that their cot is a safe environment, so that if they wake in the night or during naps it is not a daunting place to be. They will feel more comfortable, able to get back to sleep, or at least be relaxed and have some time out from stimulation.

Make a conscious effort to spend about a week taking them to the cot during the daytime – when they are wide awake, not near a sleep time. Place them in it and just do things in the room while they lie there calmly. It may be that you sit near them for 5–10 minutes, but don't give them constant attention.

Turn to them and tell them they're a clever girl/boy. Talk to them, but don't interact with them physically. Get them used to the cot as being a safe and happy place where they can be calm.

If they get upset whilst in the cot then go to them but don't pick them up. Divert their attention with something else, like a toy (no lights or sounds). You can leave this toy with them.

Increase the amount of time in the cot each day so that after a week they can do 10–15 minutes happily. As they become more comfortable with being there, reduce the light level in the room day by day so that, after a week, the light level is quite dim.

After a week to 10 days, you should find that getting them to sleep in their cot is much easier. If at any point you feel that they are getting stressed, reduce the time spent in the cot slightly until they are comfortable again, and then build on increasing the time more slowly.

Remember, the cot should NOT be a stressful place at all. Going to bed or to their bedroom must NEVER be a punishment, whether they are six months or even six years old!

I should actually call this technique of mine the Hayward Technique or the Reverse Ferber Technique. Where Richard Ferber (inventor of the Ferber method, sometimes known as the cry it out method) encourages periods of time leaving your child to cry, my technique encourages periods of time supporting your child. Here is a suggested day by day guide. If at any point your baby is stressed, take a step back to the timings on the previous day.

Day	Time to spend in cot during an awake period
1	2 minutes
2	3 minutes
3	4 minutes
4	5 minutes
5	6 minutes
6	8 minutes
7	10 minutes

WAKING UP STRAIGHT AWAY WHEN LAID DOWN

A very common problem with a few very simple solutions to fix it.

The most common cause is that your baby has not been put down to sleep at the right time. Assess their sleep cues (page 32) and try and find the optimum time to get them in their cot. Not too soon so they aren't tired enough, nor overtired, as an overtired baby will be much more resistant to being left in their cot.

Another main cause can be that they aren't placed down gently enough and their startle reflex kicks in (where they lift and stretch their arms and then bring them back closer to their body and it wakes them). Combat this being triggered by placing them down carefully and, if needs be, holding their arms gently for a few moments to prevent them from doing this. You could also try seated settling (page 123), where you place them down initially in their cot in a seated position and gradually lower them until they are lying down.

If your baby has been sleeping on you (front to front), the pressure change often wakes them. When you place them down on their back, suddenly there is no pressure on their front. Place your hand on their chest for a few moments until they relax. Also, if they have been on you, they may have been very happy cuddled up to your warm body, then when placed in a cot, it feels cold on their back. Use a hot water bottle (that has warm water in it, not hot) to warm the cot slightly beforehand. Ensure the cot doesn't get too hot. It just needs to be body temperature. Ensure that the water bottle is removed before putting the baby in the cot.

If you find that these tips aren't effective, use the plan from the previous section and try the steps again.

MAKE THEMSELVES VOMIT

This more commonly happens with toddlers. From my experience, it is generally an issue with babies that have been left to cry using cry it out methods. If you ever make the decision to leave your baby to cry for a period of time, having decided that gentle methods aren't for you, NEVER allow them to get to the point where they make themselves sick out of distress. Not only is this very upsetting for your child and you, it is also a very hard habit to get out of once they have done it. Not to mention it makes a huge mess, which is distressing for them and you.

However, if it has happened and continues to happen, there are a few steps you can take to prevent it from becoming a common occurrence. Nipping this habit in the bud quickly is very important.

Protect the cot and be prepared

Ensure that a waterproof sheet is on the cot and that you have spare bedding (sleep bag/baby clothes) close at hand.

Have a changing mat/rocker chair in the room, if possible, or a safe space you can put your baby if you have to remove them from the bed. Ensure this space is protected.

Have the floor below the cot covered with a sheet so that if your baby does vomit whilst standing up in their cot, the sheet can quickly be removed without making a mess of the floor.

Have a bin bag in the room ready to put any soiled sheets/clothing in. A pair of disposable gloves may be useful also.

Fluids (milk/water)

Reduce the amount of fluid given before a nap/night-time sleep so that if they do make themselves sick, there is less volume of liquid in the stomach.

Keep calm

If it is a small amount of vomit that can be easily wiped away, then do so and try to settle them back down. Avoid turning on all the lights or whipping them out of the cot and acting panicked. Stay as calm as possible.

If the volume of sick requires you to get your baby out of bed, use a night light only. Remove your baby and place them in the pre-prepared safe space (changing mat/rocker chair). Ensure that you calm them down with a cuddle and reassurance. Never be cross at them for vomiting.

Quickly but calmly, wearing gloves if you have them, change the bed (you should have the sheets ready). Gloves mean that once you have cleared up, you will not need to leave the room to wash your hands, and are able to simply remove them before putting your baby back in bed. Put the dirty sheets and nightwear in the bin bag you have ready, then change your baby into clean clothes.

Unfortunately if they have been sick in their hair it may require a bathroom visit which cannot be avoided.

Once your baby is clean, give them a cuddle so they are calm again and settle them back in bed. Be present in the room until they are settled. Sit on a chair or on the floor so that you are at a level below your baby. Never stand over the cot when waiting for them to settle as it will encourage them to reach up towards you, which may make them more distressed. Use the "pick up, put down" method (see page 120).

You may need to repeat this many times but do not give in. Be consistent. By doing so, you are teaching them that being sick brings them no benefit. Yes they will be cleaned up, but it doesn't mean that they get lengthy time out of their cot or can sleep somewhere else.

SEPARATION ANXIETY

Separation anxiety is where a baby suffers with anxiety when away from you or another caregiver with whom they have an emotional connection.

This can be displayed in lots of different ways, but most commonly in babies that are not speaking yet. It may be that your baby becomes very upset and distressed when you go out of sight or move away from them. Young babies are unable to understand that if you are out of sight it doesn't necessarily mean that you are not nearby. To them it feels like you are gone, and they may become distressed and cry, scream, try to follow or find you. It is very difficult for them to be comforted by someone else at the time if they have no emotional connection with them. An example of this would be when a child starts nursery and they have settling-in sessions. These allow a child to build an emotional connection with their key person and other nursery staff and children, and are generally carried out over a couple of weeks, starting with a short amount of time on day 1, sometimes with the parent being present. Day by day, the time is increased and the parent will leave the child with the nursery so that the child develops a bond. In the first few days when the parent leaves, the child often becomes very distressed. By the following week, the child will have built more of an emotional connection with their caregiver at nursery so, although they may be upset when you first leave, they will be able to be calmed by the carer much more easily. It usually takes around six weeks for a child to fully settle in a nursery setting. Some children will of course settle sooner than this, though.

For children that can speak, you may find that they shout your name when you leave, ask where you have gone or request for you to come back to them.

I find that there is a period, around 10–12 months old, where a baby begins to understand certain sequences of events. For example, if you walk towards the doorway to leave the room, they realise this means you will be gone, and they may get upset. Generally more prevalent during the daytime, this also happens around 18 months, only this time the anxiety is at its peak around bedtime, as they realise that mummy or daddy will be completely out of the room for an extended period of time once they are in bed.

I find that a few things can be put in place to reduce this anxiety.

- NEVER sneak off, even if you feel that by doing so it will bypass the anxiety of when you leave. It can actually make things worse. Always say goodbye and tell them you will be back, even if you are leaving the room momentarily.
- If you go out of sight but are still in the house with them (eg. not leaving them with someone else and going away from them), ensure that you use your voice to reassure them so they know that you are still nearby. You could carry on talking to them, tell them that you won't be long, or try singing/whistling so that they know you are near.
- Talk them through what you are doing/where you are going. No matter what age, babies are like sponges and soak up information. Even though they may not be able to speak, they can often understand a huge amount.
- With children of all ages, playing peek-a-boo can be a very effective way of teaching them that just because they cannot see you, it doesn't mean

that you are not there or available for them. It brings an element of fun to your not being able to be seen.

If your baby is still experiencing separation anxiety, particularly when placing them down to sleep for their nap or night-time sleep, it is very important to support them at this time. This is most definitely not the time to leave them crying for any period of time in the hope that they will calm down. The chances are they will not, and it may actually heighten their anxiety and make the situation worse.

TASK

As I mentioned before, moaning, protesting or shouting is OK and should be allowed. However, if they start to cry when you go to leave them try the following (in this order). If step 1 doesn't help, go onto the next, then if that step doesn't work, try the following one.

1 Reassure your baby by using your voice only to soothe them

2 Use your voice and place your hand on your baby to calm them

3 Sit next to the cot on the floor and ensure your baby is at your level. Place your hand through the cot bars and hold theirs. As they settle, withdraw your hand and use your voice to soothe them as you gradually move away. If, when you move away, they become distressed, start step 3 again.

4 If they become hysterical and your voice or touch won't calm them, pick them up and hold them firmly in your arms, rub their back or pat their back/bum and calm them down. When they are calm, tell them "it's bedtime now" and put them down in their cot again.

5 If they cry once they have settled in their cot, go back through the steps. If they get to the point of being hysterical again, keep repeating step 4. This may need much repetition, but be persistent. It may take a few nights.

NIGHT TERRORS AND NIGHTMARES

Night terrors and nightmares are very different.

NIGHT TERRORS

When a child has a night terror, they will generally be vocal when it is happening. They may shout, scream or cry (or all of them). They will likely look very disorientated and often sit up. They will not respond to you.

Night terrors usually occur during the first 3–4 hours of the night, in the NREM stages of sleep where the body can sometimes still move (unlike the REM state where the body is paralysed). Because of this, it may appear that your child is awake (sometimes their eyes may even be open), and they may throw their limbs about as if to escape from something. It usually only last a few minutes and then the child will go back to sleep and have no recollection of it in the morning.

Night terrors can happen to children of all ages but some recent research shows that they can start from around from 1.5 years old.[41]

It is unknown what specifically causes night terrors but there is no significant link between them and psychological disorders.

Research has shown that night terrors may have a slightly higher chance of occurring if certain conditions are present, such as:

Fever
Separation anxiety
Sleep deprivation
Periods of emotional stress/big changes in life
A disrupted sleep schedule
Needing to urinate

Some evidence does show that it may be genetic, so if either parent or a sibling has experienced night terrors, there is a slightly higher chance that the child will. Some disorders can also increase the chance of it happening, such as nocturnal asthma, sleep apnoea, or reflux.

Most children outgrow night terrors by the time they are 12 years old.

One's natural instinct is to wake a child if they are having a night terror, but it is best just to be close by to ensure they do not harm themselves. If they are between NREM states they may be able to hear you, so you could try and use your voice to calm them, but don't be tempted to quickly scoop them out of bed and wake them. Remember they are having a bad "dream" and picking them up may worry them further or make them fight against you. Once it has finished, they should go back to sleep with no bother.

If your child is having a night terror more than twice a week or they are causing injury to themselves, consult your doctor about it.

How to prevent night terrors

If your child has just gone through a significant life change – eg. starting nursery, a new sibling being born, or moving house – it can be enough to disrupt their sleep pattern. Allow some time for them to adjust, and ensure that everything is safe and secure within their room. If they are of an age where they can get out of their bed, make sure that any furniture is secured to the walls in case they get out of bed and are disorientated after the episode.

Go back to basics with their bedtime routine and slow things down if it has recently been rushed. Allow a good hour of wind-down time before bedtime.

If you have a child who is potty training or has bladder control, this can be a time when night terrors start. Research has shown a link between having a full bladder and their onset. If your child is suffering with night terrors then reduce the volume of liquids given before bed. In slightly older children, who may have large volumes of liquid during the day, it may be beneficial to get them to try and urinate before you go to bed. This does not mean fully waking them, but gently rousing them to encourage them to go to the toilet and then straight back to bed.

In extreme cases, some children may require further help for persistent night terrors but this is usually a last resort and only if the child is endangering themselves or it is happening so frequently that it is affecting how they are able to function the next day over a long period.

Remember, with a night terror, your child won't generally have any recollection of the bad dream, so you do not need to discuss it. Far better would be to identify a possible root cause, talking through anything they may be worried about.

NIGHTMARES

Nightmares happen in the REM state of sleep, where the body is paralysed. You will not see movement or vocalisation, and it may be that when the child wakes up they talk about it or act distressed.

Nightmares can be caused by life changes or increased stress and anxiety and are generally triggered if they see something frightening (such as a scary film on TV by accident) or even just listening in on a conversation about situations which may worry them.

As a child will only act fearful after they have woken from a nightmare, I encourage you to comfort them. Reassure them, calm them down and get them back to bed.

It may be worth having a conversation with your child the next day about their nightmare, explaining that the monster etc. wasn't real, or if they are having a nightmare about a life situation then you can talk it through with them to address their worries. I wouldn't advise talking about it too close to bedtime: better to do it when they are alert in the morning and more receptive. Also, you don't want it to be the last thing on their mind before they go to bed.

Try and use positive wording with your child. Here are a few examples when talking about things that may have a negative connotation:

Instead of using	Try	Reasoning
Oh no, it's dark	Dark time is good because it means you can have sleep time	Turning their perception of it being dark into a positive (sleep should always be talked about in a positive manner). Also, the words "oh no" communicate that what you are describing is negative.
Big spider	Look at the spider, do you think it's a baby spider or a grown-up spider?	Taking away the belief that the bigger something is, the scarier it is
That ride looks scary	That ride looks really fun	By saying "scary" it will make them think they may be harmed
That looks painful	Let's get you something to stop it hurting	Offering a solution to the problem rather than focusing on the pain

JETLAG AND CLOCK CHANGES

The changing of the clocks doesn't tend to impact a baby or child too much, but traveling through multiple time zones can have a significant impact on sleep. Babies under four months old, who have less of a feel of the difference between night and day, aren't usually affected too much. They will usually slot into the new time zone well, be that ahead or behind. For babies and children who are affected by the change of time zone, it is wise to try and keep meal times at the time of the new location as soon as possible. For example, if you are on a long flight through the night, try eating plane meals at the new time-zone mealtimes. When arriving at your destination, short naps may be needed during the daytime (if it feels like the middle of the night to them) but don't let them have a long sleep during the day or you will have a child who is wide awake half the night.

When the clocks go back, if you have a baby that wakes at 6am, it is likely that, the morning after, they will wake at 5am due to their circadian rhythm. To try and combat this, take bedtime ten minutes later every couple of days in the ten days prior to the clock change. By the time the clocks change, your child should have adjusted to the new time. You may find that when you do this, for the first few days they actually wake up slightly earlier than usual, but they will adjust.

BEDWETTING

Bedwetting is a term used in relation to a child aged five or over, who wets the bed at least once or twice a week over a three-month period.

ADH (antidiuretic hormone) is the hormone that influences urine production. This hormone isn't produced in large enough amounts until a child is generally around 3–5 years old, hence why children often still wet at night even if they are fully potty trained during the day. Night-time continence is hormone driven, so you should never punish a child for bedwetting. Until this hormone is produced, they do not have control over their urine output at night. Stress can also suppress the production of this hormone, so if a child wets the bed (even if a bit older) and is disciplined for doing so, the stress can make matters worse.

By having the understanding that night urine output is hormone driven, it takes off the pressure. Don't rush to try and get your child dry at night, as it may stress them. Signs that they may be ready to be without a nappy/pull up pants at night are: waking up totally dry in the morning, or waking in the night and asking to go to the toilet to relieve their bladder. A consistently dry nappy over the period of a week or so is what you should be looking for. The odd dry night here and there is probably coincidental, and not a sign they are ready. But it may be a sign that they are on their way to being.

If your child is over five and still persistently wets the bed, ensure you take the following steps:

- Use waterproof covers on their mattress and even their duvet.
- Have a fresh change of bedding to hand (similar to if they vomit).
- Encourage them to use the toilet before they go to bed. This may mean 5–10 minutes on the toilet to allow them time to relax. Blowing bubbles can be an effective way of making a child relax when sitting on the toilet.
- Use a reward system that is age appropriate, such as a sticker chart if they use the toilet before bed.
- Ensure they know how to get to the toilet in the night or know that if they wake and need it that they can call you and you will help.
- Reduce the amount of fluid they have in the two hours before bedtime.

Don't do the following

- NEVER punish your child if they wet the bed. Be prepared with spare clothes and bedding and make it a quick change, then straight back to sleep.
- Do not give drinks containing caffeine. These make them urinate more.
- Don't wake them regularly in the night. They will become reliant on this and it will reduce the chance of them finding the way themselves when they are ready.

If these steps do not seem to help, it may be worth speaking to your GP as it could be a sign of other things causing the bedwetting such as:

- Genetic factors – does it run in the family?
- They may sleep too deeply to wake to relieve their bladder
- Stress – try and ensure that this is reduced for the child wherever possible
- Hormonal factors – not enough ADH being produced.
- Urinary tract infections
- Abnormalities in the urethral valves in boys or in the ureter in girls or boys.
- A small bladder

Most children will be dry at night by the age of five, but there are a few who take a little bit longer. If they are not dry by aged five, it does not automatically mean that there is a problem.

Chapter 10

SLEEP DISORDERS

The sleep disorders in the previous chapter are generally grown out of and are nothing to be too concerned about. There are, however, certain sleep disorders about which you should always see a health professional.

Teeth grinding

Sometimes, when a baby is teething, they go through a temporary phase of teeth grinding which should be nothing to worry about. However, if it continues for a long period of time and becomes a regular occurrence, consult with your dentist about it. Some older children may be offered a mouthguard to prevent the grinding and causing damage to their teeth if it is persistent.

Sleep apnoea

If a baby or child has pauses in their breathing and this occurs anything from a few times in an hour up to 20 or 30 times, you should consult your doctor. Other symptoms of sleep apnoea may include:

- Difficulty staying asleep
- Extremely tired during the day
- Abrupt awakenings, then gasping for air when they wake

Children that are overweight or obese are more at risk of sleep apnoea. Other risk factors for paediatric sleep apnoea are children with enlarged tonsils or adenoids, Down's syndrome, abnormalities in the skull or face, cerebral palsy, sickle cell disease or neuromuscular disease.

Narcolepsy

This is very rare in children under seven, and usually manifests at adolescence.

Narcolepsy is very rare (0.05% of the population) with around 31,000 people affected in the UK. It is statistically even rarer in children under seven years old (approximately 10% of all cases).

Narcolepsy is generally not diagnosed until a minimum of seven years old. That being said, there have been some cases of children as young as two being diagnosed with the condition but these are extremely rare.

There are five main signs of narcolepsy, referred to using the acronym CHESS.[42]

C Cataplexy: sudden loss of muscle tone and control

H Hallucinations: vivid, dreamlike experiences that may happen when falling asleep or waking up.

E Excessive daytime sleepiness: the inability to stay awake or alert during the day. All patients with narcolepsy experience this.

S Sleep paralysis: where the body is not able to move or speak, often accompanied by hallucinations. The person suffering with this may feel that they are awake, so it can be very frightening when they feel they're unable to move.

S Sleep disruption: frequent wakes at night

Periodic Limb Movement Disorder (PLMD)

PLMD causes uncontrollable movement of the limbs. It is likely that a child suffering with PLMD will experience sleep disruption. More common in the lower limbs, it causes jerking movements of the legs (and sometimes the arms) that can disrupt the individual's sleep. Generally it will not wake the child, however it does disrupt their sleep cycles. Sleep, then, isn't as restorative as it should be, and the child will generally be very tired the next day. If your baby or child sleeps in the same room as you, you're more likely to be aware of this happening (especially if you co-sleep) or it may be something you notice on the video monitor. The jerks may happen every 20–40 seconds, in clusters which last anything from a few minutes to a few hours. The movements can be anything from full jerks of the legs (sometimes arms, but more rare) to a flex of the foot, leg kicks or brief muscle twitching. This is not to be confused with the startle (Moro) reflex, present in newborn babies or leg slamming, as mentioned on page 130.

PLMD is very similar to restless legs syndrome (RLS) where the person has an overwhelming urge to move their legs. Unlike RLS, which happens when awake, PLMD occurs when the child is asleep, so they are unaware of it.

A child suffering with PLMD may have additional symptoms such as:

- Behavioural issues
- Restless sleep
- Tossing and turning in bed
- Excessive drowsiness during the day
- Resisting bedtime

The diagnosis of PLMD would need to be carried out in a sleep clinic where movements are monitored.[43]

It is not clear what causes PLMD. Some research suggests that a lack of iron can be a contributing factor, and there are also links that caffeine and certain medications, such as antihistamines, heighten the symptoms of PLMD. Always speak with your GP if you suspect your child to have PLMD.[44]

Snoring

This one may surprise you, as snoring is quite common in adults, but how much snoring is too much and should a child snore?

The answer is that yes they may snore occasionally, especially if they have a cold and their nasal passages are congested, but if it is something that is regular (most nights), loud, and your child is sleeping with their mouth open it may be a sign of the following:

- Allergy
- Enlarged tonsils or adenoids
- Throat infection
- Sleep apnoea
- Asthma

Seek help from your GP, if your child is regularly snoring when they are not congested, to rule out any underlying issues. Snoring is more prevalent in children who are born with cleft palate or cleft lip, children who have Down's syndrome, cerebral palsy or muscular dystrophy. It is also more prevalent in children who have sickle cell disease.[45]

Chapter 11

ROUTINES

For those of you who love routines, if you feel you still need some guidance after following your baby's sleep cues, here are examples if you would prefer to be guided month by month based on a "typical" baby's sleep needs. This may seem controversial based on the title of this book, so please use as a guide on times but, most importantly, work with your baby's cues.

It is important to note that if you are breastfeeding, it should be done responsively, so that when your baby needs a feed, it should not be restricted to times dictated by the mother. Milk supply can be affected if restricted in this way. The feed timings I have stated are for a formula-fed baby – but again, feeding should never be restricted, even for them. Guidelines on formula milk are very often based on age, not weight. For this reason, I include a table of recommended amounts based on a baby's weight, rather than age. Two-month-old babies will all vary in weight, especially if they were premature. You could have a 6lb baby or a 12lb baby, and the formula milk manufacturer gives them the same guidelines as to amount!

	Recommended ounces of First Infant Milk per 24-hour period	Number of feeds	Approximate amount per feed
4lbs	10–12oz	6–8 feeds	1.5–2oz
5lbs	12–14oz	6–8 feeds	1.5–2oz
6lbs	15–17oz	6–8 feeds	1.5–2.5oz
7lbs	17–19oz	6–8 feeds	2–3oz
8lbs	20–22oz	6–7 feeds	3–4oz
9lbs	22–24oz	6–7 feeds	3.5–4oz
10lbs	24–26oz	6–7 feeds	4–4.5oz
11lbs	27–30oz	6–7 feeds	4.5–5oz
12lbs–15lbs	30–32oz	5–6 feeds	5–6oz
15lbs+	32oz	4–6 feeds	6–8oz
Over 6 months (initial weaning stages)	28oz	4–5 feeds	6–8oz
Established weaning (3 meals per day)	16–22oz	2–4 feeds	5–8oz

It is important to note that babies may not be hungry for the same amount at every single feed. As an example, if a baby has gone a long stretch throughout the night without a feed, they may be very hungry for a larger volume of milk as soon as they wake up, yet when it comes to their next milk feed a large feed may not be wanted (especially if they are eating solid food too). Be guided by your baby's needs but use the overall milk requirements for a 24-hour period to guide you. As an example, an 8 month/19lb baby may feed something like this:

7am 7oz
8am Breakfast
11am 4oz
12pm Lunch
3pm 6oz
5pm Evening meal
7pm 8oz
10/11pm 3oz dream feed
Total milk: 28oz

You can see that if you had spread the feeds more evenly, based on the 28oz recommendation for their weight, you may have fed 6oz at every feed and then a dream feed of around 4oz, yet often if the feeds are too even a baby will reject the milk, especially if they are also having solids. There is nothing wrong with feeding slightly more at one feed and a little less at another if the baby leads you this way, as long as they are having around the recommended guide of milk volume, they are gaining weight steadily, and producing 6–8 wet nappies a day.

Filling a baby up on milk unnecessarily doesn't always give a better night's sleep, and in some cases can cause digestive discomfort if they were forced to have too much.

Babies who are not weaned onto solid foods are likely to take similar amounts at most feeds, and you will find their rhythm fairly quickly.

Night weaning should be guided by your baby and never forced. It is perfectly normal for them to want to feed during the night. After around three months, if your baby is having the recommended amount of milk between the time they wake up and the time they are put to bed at night, there is no need to wake them for a feed. If however they are not gaining weight sufficiently or not producing 6–8 wet nappies in a 24-hour period, it is important to try and feed them in the night too, which may mean waking them. A lot of babies are very happy to dream feed (where a milk feed is offered to them when they are still in a sleepy state, so it isn't always necessary to fully wake them up). A baby can still suck and swallow if in a light sleep, and can do it very efficiently.

Always ensure that if you are dream feeding your baby that you aren't in a feeding position where you could fall asleep on them.

Although you may feel that the 6am wake time I have put for a baby is very early, it is in fact very normal. Please adjust accordingly for your own family dynamics, though.

MONTH 1

Month 1 will very much be a continual cycle of feeding, sleeping and small windows of awake time.

TIME	ACTION	POINTS TO NOTE
6am	Milk feed	Change baby half way through feed and wind after feed
After feed	Nap	
After sleep	Interaction	
Between 9 and 10am	Milk feed	Wind during and after feed
After feed	Take a walk to get some fresh air	May fall asleep on the walk
When home	Nap	
Between 1pm and 2pm	Milk feed	Wind during and after feed
After feed	Playtime/interaction	
When shows sleep cues	Nap	
Between 4.30pm and 5.30pm	Milk feed	Wind during and after feed
After feed	Playtime/interaction	
When shows sleep cues	Nap	
7pm	Begin wind down time. Lights dim, calm voices, warmth. Wash, massage, and change into nightwear	
Between 8pm and 9pm	Milk feed	Wind during and after feed
After feed	Time with you. Relaxing and catnapping	
At your bedtime	Milk feed	Wind during and after feed
Between 2am and 4am	Milk feed	Dim lights. Wind after feed

MONTH 2

Month 2 is very similar to month 1, but with slightly longer wake windows, and your baby will very likely be more alert. You may find that due to taking an increased volume of milk, they are able to go for longer stretches between feeds. Around 6 weeks you may notice an increased hunger, and for breastfed babies this often comes with signs, like cluster feeding where they are feeding little and often, sometimes for what might seem like hours at a time. Rest assured that as your milk supply adjusts, the feeding duration and frequency will lessen. This is a very common time for women to give up on breastfeeding as they feel that this is how it is always going to be, but it is not the case. If you do want to continue, recognise this constant feeding as a great milestone that you are achieving, and once over this frequent feeding, you and your baby will find your rhythm.

TIME	ACTION	POINTS TO NOTE
6am	Milk feed	Change baby half way through feed and wind after feed
After feed	Nap	
When they wake	Playtime/interaction	Have lots of light in the room
Between 9am and 10am	Milk feed	Change baby half way through feed and wind after feed
After feed	Nap	
When they wake	Take a walk	
Between 1pm and 2pm	Milk feed	Change baby half way through feed and wind after feed
When they show sleep cues	Nap	
Between 5pm and 6pm	Milk feed	Wind after feed
When they show sleep cues	Nap	Up to 45 minutes
After nap	Playtime/interaction	

TIME	ACTION	POINTS TO NOTE
8pm	Begin wind down time	Lights dim, calm voices, warmth. Wash, massage and change into nightwear
8.30pm	Milk feed	Wind after feed
9pm	Bedtime	
11.30pm (or around your bedtime)	Milk feed	Dim lights. Wind after feed
Between 2am and 4am	Milk feed	Dim lights. Wind after feed

MONTH 3–4

TIME	ACTION	POINTS TO NOTE
Between 6am and 6.30am	Milk feed	Change baby half way through feed and wind after feed
After feed	Nap	
When they wake	Playtime/interaction	Lots of light in the room
Between 9am and 10am	Milk feed	Wind during and after feed
After feed	Nap	
When they wake	Playtime/interaction	
Between 1pm and 2pm	Milk feed	Wind during and after feed
After feed	Nap	
When they wake	Take a walk	
Between 5pm and 6pm	Milk feed	Wind during and after feed
After feed	Nap	If they refuse this nap then bring bedtime earlier
When they wake	Playtime/interaction	Up to 45 minutes
7.30pm	Begin wind down time	Lights dim, calm voices, warmth. Wash, massage and change into nightwear
8pm	Milk feed	
8.30pm	Bedtime	
11.30pm (or around your bedtime)	Milk feed	If they do not wake for this, allow them to sleep
Between 2am and 4am	Milk feed	May still wake for this feed but if they have fed sufficiently during the day, there is no need to wake them.

MONTH 5–6

TIME	ACTION	POINTS TO NOTE
6.30am	Milk feed	Change baby half way through feed and wind after feed
After feed	Back to sleep if they want to	
8.30am/9am	Breakfast if weaning	Lots of light in the room
10am	Milk feed	Wind after feed
After feed	Playtime/interaction	
Around 11am or when they show sleep cues	Nap	
1.30pm	Milk and then lunch if weaning	Wind during and after feed
2.30pm or when they show sleep cues	Nap	
Between 5pm and 6pm	Milk feed	Wind during and after feed
After feed	Playtime/interaction	
7pm	Wind down time/ bathtime	Lights dim, calm voices, warmth. Wash, massage and change into nightwear
8pm	Milk feed	
8.30pm	Bedtime	
Around your bedtime	Dream feed if needed	If they do not wake for this, allow them to sleep
Early hours	Milk feed	May still wake for this feed but if they have fed sufficiently during the day, there is no need to wake them.

MONTH 7–9

TIME	ACTION	POINTS TO NOTE
6.30am	Milk feed	Change baby half way through feed and wind after feed
After feed	Up for the day	Lots of light in the room
8am	Breakfast	
Around 8.30am/9am or when they show sleep cues	Nap	
10am	Milk feed	Wind after feed
After feed	Playtime/interaction	
12pm	Lunch	Wind during and after feed
12.30pm/1pm or when they show sleep cues	Nap	
Between 2pm and 3pm	Milk feed	Wind during and after feed
Around 4pm or when they show sleep cues	Nap	Allow up to 1 hour
When they wake	Meal	
6pm	Bath time and then wind down	Lights dim, calm voices, warmth. Wash, massage and change into nightwear
7pm	Milk feed	Wind well after milk
After milk	Brush teeth	
7.30pm/8pm	Bedtime	
During the night	Milk feed	May still wake for this feed but if they have fed sufficiently during the day, there is no need to wake them.

MONTH 10–12

During this period, if you are finding that night-time sleep becomes a little disrupted, it may be worth trying to adjust the morning nap slightly to ensure they are not getting too much sleep during the day. However, if night-time sleep remains stable, allow your baby to lead you as 2 lengthy naps may still be appropriate for a baby until around 18 months depending on the duration of their night-time sleep. Be cautious of completely removing the morning nap too early as if they become overtired it can disrupt the night-time sleep pattern.

TIME	ACTION	POINTS TO NOTE
6.30am/7am	Milk feed	Change baby half way through feed and wind after feed
8am	Breakfast	Lots of light in the room
Around 8.30am/9am or when they show sleep cues	Nap	If night-time sleep is disrupted or bedtime becomes difficult then reduce this nap to around 45 minutes in length. Rouse your baby by making some light noise around them. Do not suddenly wake them as this can cause them to be upset upon waking.
When they wake	Milk feed	Wind after feed
After milk feed	Get out for the morning	
When home	Playtime	
12.30pm	Lunch	
When they show sleep cues	Nap	Give a small milk feed before the nap if they don't eat much lunch.
3.30pm/4pm	Try and get outside in daylight	
4.30pm/5pm	Meal	

TIME	ACTION	POINTS TO NOTE
6pm	Bath time and then wind down	Lights dim, calm voices, warmth. Wash, massage and change into nightwear
6.30pm	Milk feed	Wind well after milk
6.45pm/7pm	Bedtime	
During the night	Milk feed	May still wake for this feed but if they have fed sufficiently during the day, there is no need to wake them.

MONTHS 12–18

During this period, most babies will drop to 1 nap per day, although this time frame is a guide and you may find your baby still enjoys having 2 naps per day. Let them lead you. Signs that they may be ready to drop to 1 nap a day may include bedtime becoming difficult and them resisting going to sleep at night, total resistance to the morning nap or sudden frequent wakes at night.

TIME	ACTION	POINTS TO NOTE
6.30am/7am	Up for the day	
Upon waking	Milk feed	
After feed	Interaction	
8am	Breakfast	
At usual nap time	Restful time	During the first week of them showing signs of wanting to drop to 1 nap, allow them some quiet time in their cot or take them for a walk in the pram. Time out from stimulation can be beneficial and they may still require this restful time even if they no longer require a nap.
After the restful time	Playtime	
12pm	Lunch	Lunch earlier to allow for afternoon nap to be earlier
After lunch	Wind down ready for nap	
When they show sleep cues	Nap	Usually between 1 and 2.5 hours if no morning nap
After nap	Playtime/daylight exposure outside if possible	
4.30pm/5pm	Meal	

TIME	ACTION	POINTS TO NOTE
6pm	Bath time and then wind down and change into nightwear	
6.30pm	Milk feed	
After milk	Brush teeth	
7pm	Bedtime	If they are in the process of transitioning to 1 nap, you may find that they show sleep cues earlier than their usual bedtime. An earlier bedtime for a baby who is dropping to 1 nap, will not necessarily mean an earlier wake time the next morning.

At around 18 months, your baby will drop to one nap per day. You will know when they are ready as they will begin to resist the morning nap. If you are finding that they will just not go for their usual morning nap, don't try and force it on them. Bring what would be their afternoon nap an hour or so earlier, closer to the middle of the day, and let it extend to around 1.5–2.5 hours (don't let it be within 4 hours of bedtime.)

Bedtime during this transition time may need to be up to 30 minutes earlier than usual if they are showing sleep cues. This will adjust in time.

Around 2.5 months–3 years old, the daytime nap will begin to reduce in duration. You may find that your child just sits in their cot quite happily. This is fine, and quiet time is restful time. Once the daytime nap is dropped, bedtime may need to be tweaked.

Chapter 12

WHEN TO GET YOURSELF HELP AND WHERE FROM

There are different reasons why you may need further help.

Needing help does not mean you are any less of a parent or not doing enough for your baby. Many people experience periods of depression, anxiety or testing times related to lack of sleep. These feelings do not need to be your forever, and there is always support available.

Postnatal depression is the most common mental health disorder that women (and some men) experience after the birth of a child. As mentioned before, most women will experience the "baby blues" on day two or three after birth, which can last around a couple of weeks. This will usually subside as hormones settle. Some mothers, however, experience a more severe, longer-lasting form of depression, called postpartum depression. This is not, by any means, a sign of weakness. Treatment for postpartum depression can help manage symptoms.

If you ever feel any of these feelings listed below, PLEASE seek further help as soon as you can from your doctor or speak to a member of the family about the way you are feeling so that they can get you help if needed. If you, your partner or your child are in imminent danger, call emergency services.

- Constantly crying
- Anxiety, not just related to your baby but to other life situations too. Sometimes these situations may be minor issues, yet seem huge at the time
- A period of longer than a couple of days when you do not want to get out of bed or leave the house
- A persistent feeling of sadness or low mood
- Lack of enjoyment in the outer world
- If you are constantly getting unwell due to lack of sleep

I have spoken with many women and a few men who have suffered with postpartum depression, and I found their feelings really varied, but they have all come out the other side with help from their doctor or support network. Some phrases, when I asked them to describe how they felt, were used often, such as:

"Being unable to relax, and constantly checking the baby"
"Hurting myself and hiding it from others"
"A constant fog"
"Unable to sleep, even though the baby was sleeping"
"Feeling helpless"
"Feeling like I hated my baby"
"Separation anxiety from my baby when not holding him or with him"
"I couldn't bond, I felt like I was babysitting someone else's child"
"Feeling angry, then ashamed"
"Constantly clock-watching and not enjoying the time with my baby. Always waiting for the relief of their next nap"
"A feeling of dread"

As mentioned, postpartum depression is not a sign of weakness or a flaw in your character. There is no single cause of postpartum depression, but certain emotional and physical issues may play a role such as having a difficult pregnancy or birth, life changes that have happened, perhaps even before you got pregnant. Some mothers, who struggled with getting pregnant in the first place and may have had to have fertility treatment to conceive, have spoken to me about how they felt guilty to feel so down when their baby arrived, as they had yearned for the baby for so long. Remember that no matter how much your child is wanted, it doesn't mean you are a bad parent if you have feelings of depression once they arrive. Postpartum depression is not a reflection of how good a parent you are or how wanted and loved your baby is.

Very rarely, postpartum psychosis affects a mother after birth. This usually develops within the first two weeks of having a baby, and sometimes, but more rarely, can develop several weeks after birth. Symptoms of postpartum psychosis can include:

- Feeling confused
- Hallucinations and hearing voices

- Loss of inhibitions
- Behaving out of character
- Feeling very confused
- Delusions – thoughts that are unlikely to be true
- Manic moods – feeling high, talking or thinking too quickly

If you have postpartum psychosis, it is more likely that you will not realise, and it will be your partner, friends and family who notice the significant change. It is important that help is sought immediately via your doctor or by calling emergency services if you (or the person you suspect is suffering from postpartum psychosis) are in imminent danger of harming yourself or others. Postpartum psychosis is usually treated in hospital, ideally in a mother and baby unit, where your baby can be with you.

Your doctor

If you are experiencing symptoms of a postpartum illness, you can speak to your doctor who may be able to suggest the right type of treatment for you.

Depression is not the only form of postpartum illness. Other conditions can be triggered during pregnancy too, as well as after your baby has arrived. If you feel that you are not yourself at all after the first couple of weeks, do discuss your feelings with your doctor or you can reach out to other sources of help, which I have listed here.

Your health visitor

If you see a health visitor, reach out to them and talk with them about how you are feeling. They have a duty of care to take your concerns seriously.

Sleep consultant

Many sleep consultants will offer home visits or remote support (via video or phone call). Be sure to find out what their methods are and whether they will work for you. Most sleep consultants will offer a short phone call before signing up for a consultation package with them.

Maternity nurse

A maternity nurse can be a great support as they are trained to help, care and support, and teach you skills for your newborn baby. Their support may give you a chance to rest and recover if you are feeling sleep deprived.

Night nurse

A night nurse is very similar to a maternity nurse but will look after your baby during the night, meaning that you can get an unbroken night's sleep.

Doula

A doula is a person who supports families before, during and after birth (although some will choose to do just one or two of these). A postnatal doula is able to help and support you after birth in a non-medical capacity. They can offer great emotional support, help you care for your baby, and even support you with feeding.

Perinatal mental health team

The perinatal mental health team can be accessed via your doctor, health visitor, midwife, obstetrician or care-coordinator who will refer you to the team until your baby is one year old. They can be accessed during pregnancy and after birth. Many parents that I have worked with have found this service invaluable.

PANDAS

Offer hope, empathy and support for every parent or network affected by perinatal mental illness.
https://pandasfoundation.org.uk/

Tommy's

Mental wellbeing in pregnancy
www.tommys.org/pregnancy-information/im-pregnant/mental-wellbeing

Action on Postpartum Psychosis

A national charity for women and families affected by postpartum psychosis. Provides information and peer support, including online forums and workshops.
www.app-network.org/

BUMPS (Best Use of Medicines in Pregnancy)

Information leaflets for women and their partners about use of medication in pregnancy
www.medicinesinpregnancy.org/

Maternal OCD

Support and Information for women with Perinatal Obsessive Compulsive Disorder

www.maternalocd.org/

PND and Me

Website and online support group for sufferers of perinatal mental illness with links to information and a range of resources around this topic. Set up by a mum who had postnatal depression.

www.pndandme.co.uk/

APNI

The association for postnatal illness provides support for mothers with postnatal illness.

https://apni.org/

Bliss

Bliss support families of babies born premature or sick. They offer emotional and practical support to empower families and equip them with the knowledge and skills they need to provide the best possible care to their baby.

https://www.bliss.org.uk

Breastfeeding Support

The IBCLC (International Board of Certified Lactation Consultants) is the highest regarded professional qualification in breastfeeding knowledge and support and is recognised all over the world. To find an IBCLC near to you visit:

UK: **https://lcgb.org/find-an-ibclc/**
USA: **https://uslca.org/resources/find-an-ibclc**
Australia & New Zealand: **https://www.lcanz.org/find-a-lactation-consultant/**

You can also get support from breastfeeding peer supporters, your midwife or healthcare assistant.

UKAMB

UKAMB supports milk banks to fully implement the NICE Guidelines ensuring the distribution of safe, screened donor milk.

https://ukamb.org/

Lullaby Trust

Their mission is to reduce and prevent where possible the unexpected deaths of babies and young children and provide evidence-based knowledge to professionals, policy makers and the media to reduce the rate of unexpected deaths of babies and young children and promote child health.

https://www.lullabytrust.org.uk

Home-Start

Home-Start is a local community network of trained volunteers and expert support helping families with young children through their challenging times in the UK.

https://www.home-start.org.uk

Sands: stillbirth and neonatal death charity

Sands works to support anyone affected by the death of a baby, improve the care bereaved parents receive, and create a world where fewer babies die.

https://www.sands.org.uk/

USEFUL WEBSITES OUTSIDE THE UK

Postpartum Support International (worldwide)

Promote awareness, prevention and treatment of mental health issues related to childbearing in every country worldwide.

https://postpartum.net/

Graham's Foundation (USA)

Their vision is a world where no parent goes through the experience of prematurity alone. Their mission is to support, comfort, inform and guide families who experience a premature birth.

https://grahamsfoundation.org/

AAP (American Academy of Pediatrics)

https://www.aap.org/en-us/advocacy-and-policy/aap-health-initiatives/safe-sleep/Pages/Safe-Sleep-Recommendations.aspx

Miracle Babies Foundation (Australia)
Australia's leading organisation supporting premature and sick newborns, their families and the hospitals that care for them.
https://www.miraclebabies.org.au/

Red Nose (Australia)
Red Nose is Australia's leading authority on safe sleep and safer pregnancy advice, and bereavement support for anyone affected by the death of a baby or child.
https://rednose.org.au/section/safe-sleeping

PANDA (Perinatal Anxiety & Depression Australia)
www.panda.org.au

REFERENCES

1 https://www.lullabytrust.org.uk/professionals/statistics-on-sids/

2 https://www.jpeds.com/article/S0022-3476(05)00078-8/fulltext
Tappin, D., Ecob, R. and Brooke, H., 2005. Bedsharing, roomsharing, and sudden infant death syndrome in Scotland: a case-control study. *The Journal of Pediatrics*, *147*(1), pp.32–37.

3 https://pediatrics.aappublications.org/content/138/5/e20162938
Task Force on Sudden Infant Death Syndrome, 2016. SIDS and other sleep-related infant deaths: updated 2016 recommendations for a safe infant sleeping environment. *Pediatrics*, *138*(5).

4 NJ Scheers, Dean W. Woodard, Bradley T. Thach. Crib Bumpers Continue to Cause Infant Deaths: A Need for a New Preventive Approach, *The Journal of Paediatrics*, Volume 169, 2016, pp.93–97.

5 Guntheroth, W.G. and Spiers, P.S., 1996. Are bedding and rebreathing suffocation a cause of SIDS?. *Pediatric Pulmonology*, *22*(6), pp.335–341.

6 Gaw, C.E., Chounthirath, T., Midgett, J., Quinlan, K. and Smith, G.A., 2017. Types of objects in the sleep environment associated with infant suffocation and strangulation. *Academic pediatrics*, *17*(8), pp.893–901.
https://pubmed.ncbi.nlm.nih.gov/28723589/

7 Elliott, A.J., Kinney, H.C., Haynes, R.L., Dempers, J.D., Wright, C., Fifer, W.P., Angal, J., Boyd, T.K., Burd, L., Burger, E. and Folkerth, R.D., 2020. Concurrent prenatal drinking and smoking increases risk for SIDS: Safe Passage Study report. *EClinicalMedicine*, *19*, p.100247.

8 Thompson, J.M., Tanabe, K., Moon, R.Y., Mitchell, E.A., McGarvey, C., Tappin, D., Blair, P.S. and Hauck, F.R., 2017. Duration of breastfeeding and risk of SIDS: an individual participant data meta-analysis. *Pediatrics*, *140*(5).

9 https://doi.org/10.1136/bmj.38671.640475.55
Li, D.K., Willinger, M., Petitti, D.B., Odouli, R., Liu, L. and Hoffman, H.J., 2006. Use of a dummy (pacifier) during sleep and risk of sudden infant death syndrome (SIDS): population based case-control study. *BMJ*, *332*(7532), pp.18–22.

10 https://jamanetwork.com/journals/jamapediatrics/article-abstract/380273
Coleman-Phox, K., Odouli, R. and Li, D.K., 2008. Use of a fan during sleep and

the risk of sudden infant death syndrome. *Archives of Pediatrics & Adolescent Medicine, 162*(10), pp.963–968.

11 https://onlinelibrary.wiley.com/doi/abs/10.1046/j.1365-2222.2003.01764.x
Almqvist, C., Egmar, A.C., Hedlin, G., Lundqvist, M., Nordvall, S.L., Pershagen, G., Svartengren, M., Hage-Hamsten, M.V. and Wickman, M., 2003. Direct and indirect exposure to pets–risk of sensitization and asthma at 4 years in a birth cohort. *Clinical & Experimental Allergy, 33*(9), pp.1190–1197.

12 McGraw, K., Hoffmann, R., Harker, C. and Herman, J.H., 1999. The development of circadian rhythms in a human infant. *Sleep, 22*(3), pp.303–310.

13 Paavonen, E.J., Saarenpää-Heikkilä, O., Morales-Munoz, I., Virta, M., Häkälä, N., Pölkki, P., Kylliäinen, A., Karlsson, H., Paunio, T. and Karlsson, L., 2020. Normal sleep development in infants: findings from two large birth cohorts. *Sleep Medicine, 69*, pp.145–154.

14 Gradisar, M., Jackson, K., Spurrier, N.J., Gibson, J., Whitham, J., Williams, A.S., Dolby, R. and Kennaway, D.J., 2016. Behavioral interventions for infant sleep problems: a randomized controlled trial. *Pediatrics, 137*(6).

15 https://www.nhs.uk/live-well/sleep-and-tiredness/why-lack-of-sleep-is-bad-for-your-health/

16 Bluestone, C.D., 2005. Humans are born too soon: impact on paediatric otolaryngology. *International Journal of Paediatric Otorhinolaryngology, 69*(1), pp.1–8.

17 Souza, A.K.D.C.M., Tavares, A.C.M., Carvalho, D.G.D.L. and Araújo, V.C.D., 2018. Weight gain in newborns submitted to skin-to-skin contact.

18 https://www.sleepfoundation.org/baby-sleep/baby-sleep-cycle

19 https://www.ncbi.nlm.nih.gov/pmc/articles/PMC2140151/
Poblano, A., Haro, R. and Arteaga, C., 2008. Neurophysiologic measurement of continuity in the sleep of fetuses during the last week of pregnancy and in newborns. *International Journal of Biological Sciences, 4*(1), p.23.

20 https://journals.sagepub.com/doi/abs/10.1177/0890334415625217
Katzer, D., Pauli, L., Mueller, A., Reutter, H., Reinsberg, J., Fimmers, R., Bartmann, P. and Bagci, S., 2016. Melatonin concentrations and antioxidative capacity of human breast milk according to gestational age and the time of day. *Journal of Human Lactation, 32*(4), pp.NP105–NP110.

21 https://www.hopkinsmedicine.org/health/conditions-and-diseases/sleepwake-cycles

22 https://www.health.harvard.edu/staying-healthy/blue-light-has-a-dark-side

23 https://www.nature.com/articles/ejcn2013152#Sec6
Við Streym, S., Moller, U.K., Rejnmark, L., Heickendorff, L., Mosekilde, L. and Vestergaard, P., 2013. Maternal and infant vitamin D status during the first 9 months of infant life – a cohort study. *European Journal of Clinical Nutrition, 67*(10), pp.1022–1028.

24 https://www.emedicinehealth.com/newborn_jaundice/article_em.htm
25 https://www.sciencedirect.com/science/article/abs/pii/0022460X9190537T
26 https://www.jpma.org.pk/PdfDownload/9103
27 Honig, A.S., 1985. Singing with Infants and Toddlers.
28 https://www.nice.org.uk/guidance/ng1/chapter/1-Recommendations
29 https://www.nhs.uk/conditions/baby/weaning-and-feeding/food-allergies-in-babies-and-young-children/
30 https://www.breastfeedingnetwork.org.uk/antibiotics/
31 https://www.ncbi.nlm.nih.gov/pmc/articles/PMC5578061/
32 https://www.breastfeedingnetwork.org.uk/drugs-factsheets/
33 https://jamanetwork.com/journals/jamapediatrics/article-abstract/191516
34 https://onlinelibrary.wiley.com/doi/full/10.1002/lary.26306
35 https://link.springer.com/article/10.1007/s10911-017-9375-x
Engler, A.C., Hadash, A., Shehadeh, N. and Pillar, G., 2012. Breastfeeding may improve nocturnal sleep and reduce infantile colic: potential role of breast milk melatonin. *European Journal of Pediatrics, 171*(4), pp.729–732.
36 https://www.upi.com/Health_News/2017/01/24/Pediatricians-say-no-to-wearable-smartphone-baby-monitors/4181485293107/
37 https://safetosleep.nichd.nih.gov/research/science/backsleeping
38 https://www.ncbi.nlm.nih.gov/books/NBK542173/
Edwards CW, Al Khalili Y. Moro Reflex. [Updated 2020 Aug 30]. In: StatPearls [Internet]. Treasure Island (FL): StatPearls Publishing; 2021
39 https://onlinelibrary.wiley.com/doi/full/10.1111/apa.13124
Alm, B., Wennergren, G., Möllborg, P. and Lagercrantz, H., 2016. Breastfeeding and dummy use have a protective effect on sudden infant death syndrome. *Acta Paediatrica, 105*(1), pp.31–38.
40 http://citeseerx.ist.psu.edu/viewdoc/download?doi=10.1.1.456.6885&rep=rep1&type=pdf
Rothbart, M.K., Ziaie, H. and O'boyle, C.G., 1992. Self? regulation and emotion in infancy. *New directions for child and adolescent development, 1992*(55), pp.7–23.
41 https://jamanetwork.com/journals/jamapediatrics/fullarticle/2337224
Moreno, M.A., 2015. Sleep terrors and sleepwalking: common parasomnias of childhood. *JAMA Pediatrics, 169*(7), pp.704–704.
42 https://www.narcolepsylink.com/
43 https://my.clevelandclinic.org/health/diseases/14177-periodic-limb-movement-disorder-plmd-in-adults/management-and-treatment
44 https://www.childrens.com/specialties-services/conditions/kicking-and-or-jerky-legs-in-sleep
45 https://health.clevelandclinic.org/does-your-child-snore-5-signs-of-trouble/

GLOSSARY

Allergies: a reaction your body has to a particular food or substance

Antenatal care: the care you get from health professionals during your pregnancy

Apnoea: when breathing stops and starts while your baby sleeps

Caesarean section: also known as C-section, or caesarean delivery, is the surgical procedure by which a baby is delivered through an incision in the mother's abdomen, often performed because vaginal delivery would put the baby or mother at risk

Co-sleeping: sleeping in the same sensory space as your baby

Controlled crying: the act of leaving your baby to cry for set amounts of times or intervals until they fall asleep

Constipation: a condition in which there is difficulty in emptying the bowels, usually associated with hardened faeces

Cortisol: a hormone that regulates a wide range of vital processes throughout the body, including metabolism and the immune response. It also has a very important role in helping the body respond to stress

Cluster feeding: a time when your baby wants lots of short feeds over a few hours

Colic: when a baby has a combination of unsettled behaviours or cries a lot but there is no obvious cause.

Comforters: an item that is usually soft, such as a small piece of cloth or a soft toy that the baby finds comforting

Craniosacral therapy: a system of alternative medicine intended to relieve pain and tension by gentle manipulations of the skull regarded as harmonizing with a natural rhythm in the central nervous system

GP: a general practitioner is a medical doctor who treats acute and chronic illnesses and provides preventive care and health education to patients

Half swaddle: the practice of wrapping a baby in cloths or blankets to restrict movement of their legs, leaving their arms free

IBCLC – International Board Certified Lactation Consultant: the highest-regarded professional qualification in breastfeeding knowledge and support

Intolerance: difficulty digesting certain foods and having an unpleasant physical reaction to them

Jaundice: a medical condition with yellowing of the skin or whites of the eyes arising from excess of the pigment bilirubin and typically caused by obstruction of the bile duct, by liver disease or excessive breakdown of red blood cells

Lactose: a sugar present in milk

Lullaby Trust: a British charitable organisation aiming to prevent unexpected deaths in infancy and promote infant health

Maximum wake time: the amount of time a baby can stay awake before showing early sleep cues

Melatonin: a hormone produced in response to darkness. It helps with the timing of the circadian rhythms (24-hour internal clock) and with sleep

Moro reflex: an infantile reflex that develops between 28–32 weeks of gestation and disappears between 3–6 months of age

Mucus: a secretion of your body's mucus membranes that lubricates the inside of your body and helps protect you from bacteria

Non-REM sleep: non-rapid eye movement sleep

Oxytocin: a hormone that acts on organs in the body (including the breast and uterus) and as a chemical messenger in the brain, controlling key aspects of the reproductive system, including childbirth and lactation, and aspects of human behaviour

Postpartum: the period of time following childbirth

Premature babies: babies born before 37 weeks

REM sleep: rapid eye movement sleep

Reflux: when acid travels up the throat and into or out of the mouth

Rolling: to move from back to front or front to back

Screen-time: time on a TV/iPad/tablet

Self-settling: the act of being able to settle without assistance from a caregiver

Serotonin: the key hormone that stabilizes our mood, feelings of wellbeing, and happiness. This hormone impacts your entire body. It enables brain cells and other nervous system cells to communicate with each other. Serotonin also helps with sleeping, eating, and digestion

Shush pat: the act of using your voice to settle your baby whilst patting them rhythmically at the same time

SIDS – Sudden infant death syndrome (sometimes known as cot death) is the sudden, unexpected and unexplained death of an apparently healthy baby

Sleep association: an action that helps your baby fall asleep

Silent reflux: when acid travels up the throat but does not come into the mouth or out of the mouth. It may cause no visible symptoms

Skin to skin: the act of your baby having bare skin on their caregiver

Sleep cycles: an oscillation between the slow-wave and REM phases of sleep

Sleep latency: the time it takes to go from being awake to asleep

Special care NICU (neonatal intensive care unit) or **SCBU** (special care baby unit). Specialist care for premature or unwell babies

Swaddling: the practice of wrapping a baby in cloths or blankets to restrict movement of their arms and legs

Teething: the process of growing or cutting milk teeth

Tongue tie: where the strip of skin connecting the baby's tongue to the bottom of their mouth is shorter than usual

Transition to cot: the act of moving your child into their own cot or the act of moving your child from being in arms into their cot

Twins and multiples: two or more babies born from the same pregnancy

Vomiting: eject the contents of the stomach through the mouth

Weaning: the process of gradually introducing an infant to what will be its adult diet

INDEX

Printed in Great Britain
by Amazon

77119278R00120